Essential Evidence-Based Teaching Strategies

Garry Hornby • Deborah Greaves

Essential Evidence-Based Teaching Strategies

Ensuring Optimal Academic Achievement
for Students

 Springer

Garry Hornby 🆔
Institute of Education
University of Plymouth
Plymouth, UK

Deborah Greaves
Learning Across Boundaries Consulting Ltd
Atlanta, GA, USA

ISBN 978-3-030-96231-9   ISBN 978-3-030-96229-6   (eBook)
https://doi.org/10.1007/978-3-030-96229-6

This Springer imprint is published by the registered company Springer Nature Switzerland AG
The registered company address is: Gewerbestrasse 11, 6330 Cham, Switzerland

This book is dedicated to our combined families who have given their quiet support and patience as we worked to compile this book. To the many teachers working against challenging situations as schools worldwide continue to deliver effective instruction following a pandemic, we hope that this book will be useful to you in supporting your students and improving their educational outcomes.

Foreword

Teachers who are serious about wanting to teach effectively, to do their job to the very best of their ability, will love this book. By being serious about teaching I mean actually doing it very well, not just having the right "philosophical" ideas or attitudes that are based more on speculation, usually called "theory," than reliable empirical evidence.

It is refreshing to see a book about teaching that is based on empirical evidence, not philosophy or speculation. One of the great things about this book is that it gets to some of the nitty-gritty of teaching, how to do it well from a practical standpoint. Its message to teachers is this: If you do not get instruction right, then you limit your effectiveness and everything else, including behavior management, falls apart. The book emphasizes that it is important how teachers talk to students, how they relate to them on a personal level, and how students are grouped for instruction. These are critical factors because the details of teaching are not incompatible with using effective instructional tools. Rather, they enhance the tools of instruction and teachers' relationships with students.

Instruction that is direct and follows rules and predictable patterns is not necessarily "mechanical" or "uncreative." Being sensitive to students' individuality requires creativity as well as competence in the skills discussed in this book.

Hornby and Greaves capture in ten chapters the attitudes and tools successful teachers need. All educators need these skills and, at the same time, must recognize the fact that although they are backed by critical evidence, all have their limitations and boundaries. Some of these limitations, contingencies, or boundaries seem obvious, such as that applying evidence-based practices too mechanically will limit their effectiveness. For example, peer tutoring, used by itself or within cooperative learning, may well be supported by extensive research findings. However, that does not mean that *any* age peer can be an effective tutor or that peer tutors can always be effective without training or guidance. Also, although ability grouping has its limits and boundaries and may well be an ineffective procedure as typically practiced, that does not mean that effective teaching may be achieved by grouping students willy-nilly. Mixing students who are starkly different in ability and paying little or no attention to the size of the group or range of abilities are prescriptions for instructional disaster, no matter how good the teacher is. The grouping of students needs to be more strategic, as suggested in the book.

An important concept for educators at all levels is this: Nothing *always* works, and everything *appears* to have worked at least once. This makes it possible for critics of *any* teaching procedure to point to its failures and, therefore, condemn it. It also makes it possible for the advocates of *any* teaching procedure to claim success, even though the procedure they recommend is not based on the accumulation of empirical evidence but, instead, relies on testimonial evidence. This is an old, sad trap that hamstrings many teachers.

Hornby and Greaves recommend and describe the procedures that will *usually, most often* lead to students' learning. Part of the art and science of teaching is recognizing and implementing the procedures offering the highest probability of success. To this end, Hornby and Greaves highlight those teaching procedures most likely to work and provide detailed guidelines for their effective implementation, usefully complemented by links to videos of their use in real-life classrooms.

University of Virginia   James M. Kauffman,
Charlottesville, VA, USA

Foreword

Evidence—the latest buzzword in education! Some legislation insists that everything must be evidence-based; there are so many who claim that their methods are evidence-based, and there are many websites, depositories, and organizations that promote their evidence base. My work is based on a third of a million students, so do we really need more evidence? Perhaps, the days of collecting and disseminating evidence are over. The core issue rather is the mobilization and utilization of evidence-based methods—and that is the essence of this book.

This book starts from the premise that evidence-based practice signifies practices and programs shown by high-quality research to have meaningful effects on student outcomes. The two keywords are *high quality* and *meaningful*, and what I find fascinating is that across the many implementations of evidence-based methods (outlined in the first chapter), there is a remarkable consistency as to the methods that qualify.

If we set the bar so, can these interventions improve learning? Then almost everything works! So, providing evidence of improvement is not enough. Hence, in this book, the bar is raised to "meaningful" and while wise, this asks for evidence that the intervention is indeed impactful in a meaningful manner on each child. There are many forms of evidence that are high quality and meaningful—the noticing, the observations, the judgements by teachers during lessons, the interpretations for the artifacts of student work, the listening to how students are processing information and learning, the information from assignments and assessments, and much more. These too need to be high quality, and particularly the interpretations from the evidence within classes need to be checked for validity, consistency, and triangulation. Evidence is not the exclusive domain of the academic, Google Scholar, or journals. Indeed, many of the "evidence-based" practices employ and often depend on teacher's interpretations, fidelity of implementation, and relentless focus on the teacher's impact to be successful in the class.

Hence, the emphasis is on each teacher "knowing their impact" on each student and choosing interventions that make this evidence meaningful. A tough ask. However, there are interventions that have the probability of this level of impact. But note the key word probability. Past evidence leads to probabilities not actualities. And it is the moment-by-moment observing and decision-making, the stopping to evaluate the impact, the listening to the sound of learning, the skill in analyzing patterns of behaviors, and the differentiation when choosing optimal interventions that provide evidence that also need to be checked, critiqued, and evaluated.

Hornby and Greaves choose eight high-probability interventions, and these need to be in the tool kit of every teacher. They start by asking about the climate of the class. Building relations between teachers and students, and between students, is the baseline—without a sense of being invited to learn, safe in acknowledging not knowing and making errors, and without the sense of joy and wonder at discovery and learning, then for many students, it is all over and compliance (at best), survival, or turnoff (at worst) are the probable outcomes.

Like Hornby and Greaves, I go back to Carl Rogers for the seminal findings on developing climate—and his powerful arguments about listening—not only active listening by the teachers but also teaching students how to actively listen. It may mean teachers showing students that they too can listen, as listening is the core skill in formative assessment, peer tutoring, behavior assessment, and parent engagement. Active listening not only shows a genuineness to the students about caring for their learning improvement, but also shows students that they are listening to how teachers can enhance their clarity and credibility.

The best way to maintain great classroom environments is to engage in, promote, and esteem learning. This builds the teacher's credibility in the eyes of students and is what leads to higher levels of engagement. This is how we teach students the metacognitive skills to become their own teachers. Peer tutoring is but one way to then use these skills as a teacher, as are exit tickets (Can you now teach someone else?). These methods help consolidate the learning and teach students how to stand in the shoes of others and see how their peers think and process (a core skill of all teachers). And we do this via formative evaluations, direct instruction (often misunderstood, so this chapter is a necessary reading), and functional behavior assessment.

Not all students, all the time, wish to engage in the learning and discovery in our classrooms, and Hornby and Greaves use their depth of skill and background experience of this method to illustrate the power of foundational behavioral assessment. Equally with parents—I have rarely met a parent who does not want to help their child with their schooling, but many do not have the skills (which is why we have schools). The theme in this chapter is sharing the language of learning with the parents, listening to their queries, and building trust that their child is gaining more than a year's value for the year in your classroom.

They end this book with a discussion of why evidence-based teaching methods do not always get implemented—in medicine as well as in schools. Surely, we would want our doctors to wash their hands before they touch and prod us; surely, we want our teachers to implement the methods most probable to help children learn. Surely, we want our doctors to be proud that they read and keep up to date with improved and powerful methods and do not rely on the methods they like and that have worked in the past and not rely on methods they have so often used. This applies equally to teachers.

My view is that the reticence of some educators to adopt high-probability evidence-based methods relates to our theories of change and improvement in the classroom. We build theories by seeking evidence, we have massive confirmation bias to see success when we have implemented our favorite methods, and we have many explanations why students cannot learn. Hence, we need not rush and adopt methods like the eight in this book, until we ask: How effective and efficient are we with all our students? Are we prepared to be wrong in the methods we have been using (and how would we know this)? Are we willing to see the impact of high-probability methods to then add to our tool kit? All this requires an openness to evidence of our impact, collegial support, and critique to review our impact when using these methods (compared to our previous methods), and formative evaluation skills to know when is the right time, for the right students, for the right amount of implementation.

Here is where this book is so powerful.

Melbourne Graduate School of Education   John Hattie
University of Melbourne,
Melbourne, Australia

Preface

The motivation for producing this book has come about from two unrelated developments that have occurred in the last 20 years. Without these, the book would just not have been possible. First is the rapid growth in research evidence for the effectiveness of teaching strategies in the field of education. This is reinforced by the creation of sources, where this evidence has been analyzed, summarized, and brought together in forms that are easily accessible to teachers. Second is the rapid growth in the popularity and use of freely available internet services, such as YouTube, that store and present videos to share information on a wide range of topics, including those that are useful to teachers. This provides a means for educators to not only learn about new teaching strategies but also see them in action by watching videos of them being used in real-life classrooms.

So, this combination of developments presented us with a possible solution to our frustration with the current speed of progress toward the uptake of evidence-based teaching strategies and the establishment of an evidence-based approach in education.

The book makes a case for the widespread use of evidence-based practice in education and identifies eight key evidence-based teaching strategies that teachers have control over and can implement in their classrooms. The book is relevant to both newly qualified teachers and practicing teachers who can all improve their practice by learning how to effectively identify and implement evidence-based teaching strategies. This will ensure that effective teaching strategies are embedded in the daily practice of teachers and schools.

This book is intended for use in initial teacher education and in-service training of teachers at all levels, from early childhood education through secondary school teaching. However, the book has been designed so that it can also benefit individual teachers or small groups of teachers, at any stage of their careers, by enhancing their knowledge of evidence-based strategies and providing guidance on implementing these in their classrooms. It is intended that using the book in this way, as well as during formal teacher education and training, will lead to teaching becoming a more evidence-based profession, which will result in improved educational outcomes at all levels of education systems.

Plymouth University   Garry Hornby
Plymouth, UK

Acknowledgments

We would particularly like to thank Dr. Marcia Pilgrim for sharing her professional insight to ensure that the content of the book is "teacher-friendly." Her substantive feedback on the earlier drafts of the chapters was invaluable. We would also like to thank Philippa Gordon for carefully proofreading the final draft and giving us some useful feedback. We much appreciate Judy Jones of Springer for being so understanding about the delay in completing the book. In Barbados in 2020, we have had a Category 1 hurricane and volcanic ash fall from St. Vincent, on top of battling the COVID-19 pandemic. To finish the book has truly been a cooperative effort and a great example of the "positive interdependence," which is discussed in the book.

Contents

1 Importance of Evidence-Based Teaching Strategies 1
Rationale for the Book 1
Importance and Challenges of Using Evidence-Based Teaching
Strategies. 2
Sources of Evidence-Based Practice. 4
Example of Evidence from the Above Sources on a Well-Known
Intervention. 6
Interventions That Are Not Evidence-Based Practices. 6
    Ability Grouping. 7
    Learning Styles 8
    Irlen Lenses. 8
Key Evidence-Based Practices for Education. 9
Conclusion 11
References. 11

2 Teacher-Student Rapport. 15
Rationale 15
Listening Skills 17
    Attentiveness. 17
    Passive Listening. 18
    Paraphrasing 19
    Active Listening 19
Assertion Skills. 20
    Basic Elements of Assertiveness. 20
    Giving Constructive Feedback 21
    Responding to Criticism 22
    Dealing with Aggression. 23
    Problem-Solving. 24
Teaching Programs of Social and Emotional Development 25
    Circle Time 25
    Incredible Years Programs 26

Teacher Skills for Leading Social and Emotional Learning Programs. .   27
Conclusion   28
References.   28

3   Formative Assessment.   31
Rationale   31
Theory.   32
Performance Feedback   33
Formative Assessment Practices.   34
    Planning   34
    Frequency and Timing   34
Using Formative Assessment Information   35
    Setting Goals for Learning: Where Is the Learner Going?.   35
    Monitoring the Learner: Where Is the Learner Functioning Now? . .   35
Practices That Support Formative Assessment   36
    Observation.   36
    Questioning.   37
    Self-Reflection   37
    Criterion-Based Assessments   38
    Cooperative Learning Strategies.   38
Formative Assessment Strategies for Preschool and Elementary
Students.   39
    Experiential Learning with Targeted Observation   39
Strategies for Middle and High School Students   40
    Rubrics   40
    Entrance and Exit Tickets   41
    Checklists   41
Conclusion   42
References.   42

4   Direct Instruction   45
Rationale.   45
Historical Development   46
Overview of Direct Instruction Programs.   47
    Published Programs   47
Principles of Direct Instruction.   48
Classroom Practices   49
Planning for Instruction   49
    Students' Existing Knowledge and Skills.   51
    Engaging Students   52
    Adapting to the Needs of Older Students   52
During the Lesson.   53
    Setting Learning Intentions.   53
    Scaffolded Instruction.   53
    Demonstration and Modeling   54
    Guided Practice.   55

Independent Practice. 56
Feedback and Verification. 56
Direct Instruction Strategies for Preschool and Elementary Students . . 57
Reading Recovery. 58
Shared Reading. 59
Strategies for Middle and High School Students 59
Scaffolding with Socratic Circles 59
Explicit Instruction 60
Conclusion 60
References. 61

5   Cooperative Learning. 63
Rationale. 63
Theory. 64
Positive Interdependence 65
Group Sharing. 66
Role-Playing 66
Individual Accountability 66
Group Recitation of a Poem or Oral Retelling of a Story. 67
Group Study with Random Checking. 67
Face-to-Face Promotive Interaction 67
Blind Drawing. 68
Parking Lot 68
Social Skills 68
Activities to Encourage Participation, Turn-Taking,
and Respect-Building Skills 69
Group Processing 70
Planning for Cooperative Instruction 70
Selecting Assignments 71
Purpose of Groups. 72
Factors to Consider When Forming Groups 72
Rewarding in a Cooperative Environment 73
Establishing Work Habits and Behaviors 73
Making Cooperative Learning Strategies Part
of Classroom Routines 75
Cooperative Learning Strategies for Elementary Students. 75
Numbered Heads Together 75
Four Corners 76
Cooperative Learning Strategies for Middle and High
School Students. 77
Jigsaw 77
Student Teams Achievement Divisions (STAD). 77
Group Investigation. 78
Conclusion 78
References. 79

6 Peer Tutoring 83
Rationale 83
Theory 84
Peer Tutoring Models 84
Planning for Peer Tutoring 84
Building Effective Peer Tutoring Teams 86
  Creating an Appropriate Climate of Sharing 87
  Establishing Learning Structures to Improve Knowledge
  and Accuracy 87
  Identifying Learning Outcomes 87
  Clarifying Tutoring Methods 88
  Monitoring Progress and Providing Feedback 88
Peer Tutoring Strategies for Elementary Students 89
  Class-Wide Peer Tutoring 89
  Reciprocal Peer Tutoring 90
Peer Tutoring Strategies for Secondary Students 90
  Peer-Assisted Learning Strategies (PALS) 90
  Peer Editing 91
Conclusion 92
References 92

7 Metacognitive Strategies 95
Rationale 95
Theory 96
Study Skills 96
  Concept Mapping 96
  Mnemonics 97
  SQ3R Reading Method 98
  Reciprocal Teaching 99
  KWL 100
  Anticipation Guide 101
  Think Aloud 101
  Additional "Think-Aloud" Tips 102
Conclusion 102
References 103

8 Functional Behavior Assessment 105
Rationale 105
Theory 107
Preventative Measures 107
  School-Wide Supports 108
  Classroom Supports 108
  Individual Supports 110
Conducting a Functional Behavior Assessment (FBA) 111
  Involving Parents, Teachers, Students, and Relevant Staff ... 111
  Functional Analysis 111

Descriptive Assessment.. 112
Indirect Assessment 113
Developing Behavior Intervention Plans (BIP) 114
Implementing the BIP.. 114
Monitoring and Modifying the BIP 114
Strategies for Preschool and Elementary Students 115
Visual Schedules.. 115
Check-in and Checkout.. 115
Strategies for Middle and High School Students 116
The Student-Teacher Game..................................... 116
Behavior Contracts 116
Conclusion 117
References.. 118

9   Parental Engagement 121
Rationale... 121
Barriers to Effective Parent Involvement 122
Theoretical Approach to Facilitating Effective Parent Engagement.... 123
Parental Needs 123
Parental Contributions.. 124
Strategies and Interventions for Effective Parental Engagement 126
Strategies for Encouraging Parents into School 126
Parent-Teacher Meetings...................................... 126
Written Communication 127
Telephone Contacts... 127
Technological Options for Communication 128
Home Visits.. 128
Attitudes and Beliefs on Working with Parents 128
Examples of PI and PE at Various Stages of the Education System.... 129
Early Years Examples 129
Elementary School Examples.................................. 130
Middle School Examples 130
High School Examples 130
Conclusion 131
References.. 131

10 Implementation of Evidence-Based Teaching Strategies........... 133
Rationale for Focusing on Implementation...................... 133
Barriers to the Use of Evidence-Based Strategies 134
Factors Facilitating the Use of Evidence-Based Teaching Strategies... 136
Sustaining the Use of Evidence-Based Teaching Strategies.......... 137
Conclusion 138
References.. 139

Index... 141

About the Authors

Garry Hornby (BSc, MA, Dip.Ed.Psych., PhD, CPsychol., FBPsS) is an Emeritus Professor of Education at the Institute of Education at the University of Plymouth in the UK. Garry was born in England and completed a degree in physics at the University of Leeds. His first job was as a counselor/care worker in a residential school for emotionally disturbed and intellectually disabled children in the USA. He then worked as a secondary school teacher of mathematics and science in England and New Zealand. From there, he went on to teach a special class for children with moderate learning difficulties in Auckland and was subsequently trained as an educational psychologist at the University of Auckland. He worked as an educational psychologist and then a teacher educator at the Auckland College of Education, before returning to England. He then worked as a lecturer and researcher at the Universities of Manchester and Hull, where he obtained his PhD. He also worked as a consultant on special needs education for the Ministry of Education and lectured for 2 years at Erdiston College and the University of the West Indies in Barbados. In 2002, he moved to Christchurch, New Zealand, where he was a Professor of Education at the University of Canterbury for 12 years. During 2016 and 2017, he was the Director of Research at the Institute of Education at the University of Plymouth in the UK. He is married to a Barbadian, and they have two adult sons, now living in Barbados.

Garry's teaching and research are in the areas of educational psychology, special education, counseling and guidance, teacher education, and parental involvement in education. He has published over 200 journal articles and book chapters and 13 books in the field of education, including *Counselling in Child Disability* (Chapman and Hall, 1994); *Improving Parental Involvement* (Cassell, 2000); *Mental Health Handbook for Schools* (Routledge. 2002); *Counselling Pupils in Schools: Skills and Strategies for Teachers* (Routledge, 2003); *Meeting Special Needs in Mainstream Schools* (second ed.) (David Fulton, 2000); *Parental Involvement in Childhood Education: Building Effective School-Family Partnerships* (Springer, 2011); and *Inclusive Special Education: Evidence-Based Practices for Children with Special Needs and Disabilities* (Springer, 2014).

Deborah Greaves (BSc, MEd, EdS, EdD) is an educator with over 30 years of experience at elementary, secondary, and tertiary levels. Upon completion of secondary school in Barbados, Deborah pursued studies at the University of Pittsburgh, receiving her first degree in child and adolescent development, followed by studies in language and learning disabilities at York University in Canada under a Canadian Commonwealth Fellowship award. Upon completion of a master's degree, Deborah returned to Barbados to serve as a Tutor at Erdiston College and did a 2-year tenure of service at St. Gabriel's School and Codrington High School.

Later returning to the USA, Deborah worked as a teacher, professional development trainer, and special education supervisor with two of the larger school districts in Atlanta, Georgia. Her responsibilities encompassed classroom instruction, providing instructional support and coaching to teachers, and teacher mentoring and training. In her most recent position with DeKalb County Schools in Georgia, she provided support to multiple schools on matters pertaining to special education instruction, teacher training, and legal compliance with special education mandates. During these tenures, Deborah earned her doctoral degree in educational leadership at the University of Georgia. Her recent research has focused on how teachers apply their knowledge to improve students' academic achievement - *Data use practices at Newbury Charter: Using an action research approach to examine and inform practices (2018)*. Previous research projects included studies of West Indian students in Canadian classrooms - *Teaching students placed in second dialect classes: An analysis of teachers' perceptions of success (1988)*.

Deborah has presented modules on Collaborative Coaching and Classroom Management, across Atlanta and notably at a National Staff Development Council Conference in Denver, Colorado. She is a certified trainer for the Anti-Defamation League and has conducted presentations and training seminars with students, parents, and teachers on issues related to diversity in education, anti-bullying, and anti-hate practices in schools. She currently works as an education consultant with interests in education policy, teacher preparation, instruction for diverse learners, and special education advocacy.

Chapter 1
Importance of Evidence-Based Teaching Strategies

Abstract The thesis of this book is that a critical component of effective education is the use of teaching strategies that have strong bases of research evidence. Successful implementation of evidence-based practice requires that teachers use instructional strategies that have proven effectiveness and avoid those that do not. Therefore, teachers need to have a clear understanding of precisely what evidence-based practice actually means, and how it is different from other terms, such as research-informed practice, which is less precise and rigorous. Effective evidence-based strategies require strong research evidence, teacher wisdom and skills, and alignment with school and community cultures. The most useful sources of information on the evidence bases supporting educational strategies and large-scale syntheses of meta-analyses are identified. In addition to using evidence-based strategies, teachers need to be able to recognize and avoid interventions that are not evidence-based. An example of a well-established evidence-based intervention is presented and three examples of interventions that are not evidence-based are identified. Eight interventions that are considered to be key evidence-based strategies for improving student outcomes are identified and these are discussed in subsequent chapters of this book.

Rationale for the Book

The importance of collecting data and using evidence to improve the effectiveness of practice in fields such as medicine and agriculture has been accepted for over 100 years. One example of this is the more than quadruple increase in the quantity of milk produced per year by dairy cows over the period of the previous century (Vande Harr & St. Pierre 2006). In contrast, in education, despite going from mainly primary school attendance in 1900 to nearly universal access to secondary education by 2000, there was little increase in standards of literacy and numeracy. In fact, standards of literacy and numeracy remain of international concern, despite numerous policies and intervention programs aimed at improving this situation. Slavin (2008) considered that the contrast between improvements in education and those in agriculture and other fields is due to differences in the implementation of evidence-based practice.

A critical component of effective education is considered to be the use of teaching strategies that have strong bases of research evidence for their effectiveness as well as the avoidance of those that lack such evidence (Hattie 2009; Marzano 1998; Slavin 1996). While there have been criticisms of the evidence-based practice approach in education on both theoretical (Biesta 2010; Hammersley 2013) and methodological grounds (Pampaka, Williams & Homer 2016; Simpson 2017), there is now overwhelming support for its importance in improving educational outcomes (Cook, Tankersley and Landrum 2016; Gorard, See & Siddiqui 2017; Higgins & Katsipataki 2016). There is also general awareness of the challenges involved in ensuring the widespread use of evidence-based teaching strategies in education systems (Green, Taylor, Buckley & Hean 2016; Hornby, Gable & Evans 2013).

An important factor in the successful implementation of evidence-based practice is that teachers need to make sure that they use instructional strategies that have proven effectiveness and avoid those that do not, in order to optimize student outcomes (Hornby et al. 2013). Therefore, teachers need to be able to evaluate strategies, interventions, and programs in terms of the adequacy of their research bases, so that they can select those that are evidence-based practices and avoid those that are not. They also need to know how to overcome various barriers to the implementation of such interventions in classrooms in order to embed evidence-based strategies into the culture and everyday practice of schools. These issues are addressed below, and eight well-established evidence-based strategies for effective teaching, that are considered key to implementing evidence-based practice, are identified.

Importance and Challenges of Using Evidence-Based Teaching Strategies

In the past three decades, there has been an exponential increase in research evidence collected on the effectiveness of strategies, interventions, and programs used in the field of education (for example see Hattie 2009). What many experts in the field bemoan is that this has largely *not* been translated into day-to-day practice in schools. That is, despite having clear evidence for the effectiveness of some strategies, but not others, this has not resulted in widespread changes to the educational practice of teachers (Brown 2013; Burns & Ysseldyke 2009; Cook et al. 2016; Gorard et al. 2017).

The field of educational research has seen a progression over time in its demands for more rigorous research evidence, which has been reflected by changes in the terminology used. Thirty years ago, terms such as "best practice" were used to describe strategies that were thought to be effective, which may have had some research evidence supporting them (see Hornby, Atkinson & Howard 1997). Then the term "research-based" emerged to denote practices supported by the balance of research evidence, whereas practices with substantial research evidence for their effectiveness were often referred to as "empirically supported" or "empirically validated" (Cook & Cook 2011). In the last decade, the term "evidence-informed practice" has become widely used for referring to approaches that are informed by research, without indicating the rigor or extensiveness of this research evidence.

More recently, the term "evidence-based practice" has emerged to signify, "practices and programs shown by high-quality research to have meaningful effects on student outcomes" (Cook & Odom 2013, p. 136). This is a much more stringent benchmark than the terms "best practice" or "research-informed" in that it requires the evidence to be based on extensive rigorous research having been conducted, and also requires that the impact on outcomes is substantial and meaningful. However, teachers may assume that interventions referred to as "research informed" are underpinned by solid research evidence, while this need not be the case. Research informed can mean just about anything, including being based on a single piece of research or based on research of dubious quality or that is disseminated by promoters of recommended interventions in which they have a vested interest. Therefore, teachers need to have a clear understanding of precisely what evidence-based practice actually means, and how it is different from similar sounding terms, before they can be expected to commit to using them in their classrooms.

From an evidence-based practice perspective, in order to be optimally effective, teachers need to be aware of the research evidence for the instructional strategies that they use. Wherever possible, teachers need to use strategies for which solid research evidence of effectiveness has been established. That is, they need to use mainly evidence-based strategies (Cook & Cook 2011; Cook et al. 2016). When considering using instructional strategies, teachers need to be aware that some of them will have well-established extensive evidence bases and be considered evidence-based practices, such as formative assessment (Hattie & Timperley 2007). Other strategies will have some evidence for their effectiveness and may be considered research-based, such as Circle Time (Canney & Byrne 2006). There are still others that are promising strategies that have not yet established an extensive evidence base, such as the flipped classroom approach (DeLozier & Rhodes 2017). Teachers will also come across interventions and programs that have extremely limited evidence of effectiveness but which still continue to be used, such as ability grouping (Hornby & Witte 2014), or even strategies that have convincing evidence that they are ineffective or harmful, such as facilitative communication (see Hornby et al. 1997). Determining which category each intervention falls into is considered an essential first step in planning instructional strategies to be used in the classroom.

However, having a strong base in research evidence is not the only consideration when selecting instructional strategies. Educational strategies also need to be implemented within the current context and practical realities of schools and classrooms. They are highly dependent on professional wisdom built on extensive teaching experience (Cook & Cook 2011). Educational interventions also need to be culturally appropriate and fit with parents' and teachers' values, knowledge, skills, and experience, and those of families and communities (Habib, Densmore-James & Macfarlane 2013). As clarified by Schlosser and Sigafoos (2008, p.61),

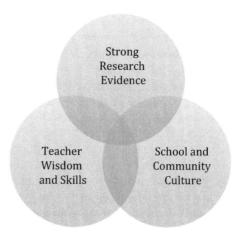

Fig. 1.1 Components of Effective Evidence-Based Practice

"Evidence-based practice is commonly understood to be the integration of the best and most current research evidence with clinical expertise and relevant stakeholder perspectives." Thus, effective evidence-based practices occur at the convergence of extensive research evidence of meaningful change, relevant teacher wisdom and skills, as well as consistency with school and community cultures, as illustrated in Fig. 1.1.

Sources of Evidence-Based Practice

Research evidence for the effectiveness of interventions can now be found in a wide range of sources, including articles reporting individual studies and reviews, meta-analyses, and syntheses of the research literature. Four of the most useful sources of information on the evidence bases supporting educational strategies and interventions are large-scale syntheses of meta-analyses, such as those by Hattie (2009) and the Teaching and Learning Toolkit, as well as those provided by the Best Evidence Encyclopedia and the What Works Clearinghouse.

Hattie (2009) published a synthesis of over 800 meta-analyses relating to achievement in the field of education, from which he found 0.4 to be the average effect size for educational interventions. *Hattie's synthesis of meta-analyses* is regularly updated online. He reported that an effect size larger than 0.4 indicates above-average impact of the intervention and is therefore important to consider when selecting teaching strategies. Hattie rank ordered the effect sizes of interventions included in his synthesis, so that it is easy to see which ones have above-average and which have below-average impacts. For example, a selection of effect sizes reported are as follows: formative assessment: 0.90; student-teacher relationships: 0.72; cooperative (versus individual) learning: 0.59; homework: 0.29; ability grouping: 0.12; and retention in grade: –0.16. These findings indicate that the use of formative assessment, enhanced student-teacher relationships, and cooperative learning are all interventions that are effective. Therefore, they are considered evidence-based strategies and should be widely used in schools. It also suggests that homework and use of between-class ability grouping are less effective and are therefore not recommended. Further, that retaining students in a grade is likely to have a negative impact on educational achievement, and is definitely not an evidence-based practice, so should be avoided.

The Teaching and Learning Toolkit was developed by the Education Endowment Foundation (EEF), an independent grant-making charity, initially funded by the UK Department for Education, dedicated to raising the educational achievement of children and young people. The EEF invests in evidence-based projects which focus on evaluating interventions using randomized controlled trials or quasi-scientific designs. The results of these evaluations are included in the *Teaching and Learning Toolkit*. This provides a summary of evidence on a range of interventions, so that schools have rigorous evidence on which to base their choice of teaching strategies and programs. For each of the interventions, the Toolkit provides ratings of cost-effectiveness, strength of the research evidence, and size of the impact. For example, "Feedback" is rated as having a high impact for low cost, based on a moderate amount of evidence, and can therefore be considered an evidence-based practice. "Metacognition" is rated as having a high impact for very low cost, based on extensive evidence, and can also be considered an evidence-based practice. "Learning Styles" is rated as having low impact for very low cost, based on limited evidence, and "Setting or Streaming" is rated as having a negative impact for very low cost, based on moderate evidence. Therefore, neither of these two interventions is considered to be an evidence-based practice.

The *Best Evidence Encyclopedia* is a website that includes research syntheses on many topics. It was founded with funding from the U.S. Department of Education and aimed to provide educators and researchers with information about the strength of the evidence supporting various educational interventions. The Best Evidence Encyclopedia provides summaries of scientific reviews produced by many authors and organizations and links to the full texts of each review. The reviews selected for inclusion in the Best Evidence Encyclopedia are meta-analyses or syntheses that apply rigorous scientific standards to bodies of evidence that meet high standards of methodological quality of programs currently available to educators. Educational interventions are rated as having either strong, moderate, limited, or no evidence of effectiveness, as determined by average effect sizes found in the studies included in syntheses. In contrast to Hattie's average of 0.4, because the Best Evidence Encyclopedia includes only research with the most rigorous methodology, reported effect sizes of over 0.25 are considered to be educationally meaningful (Slavin 1996), so interventions with reported effect sizes on the Best Evidence Encyclopedia of over 0.25 can be considered to be evidence-based practices.

The *What Works Clearinghouse* is a branch of the U.S. Department of Education Institute of Education Sciences. The What Works Clearinghouse compiles reviews of research articles that have examined the efficacy of instructional or intervention approaches. It conducts rigorous reviews of each article following a detailed evaluation of methodology and then summarizes the strength of the scientific support for the approach. The What Works Clearinghouse has rigorous inclusion criteria and only includes educational interventions with the most rigorous research evidence supporting their effectiveness. Therefore, interventions included in the What Works Clearinghouse, such as Reading Recovery, which is discussed below, are considered to be evidence-based practices.

Example of Evidence from the Above Sources on a Well-Known Intervention

Reading Recovery was developed during the 1970s in New Zealand by Professor Dame Marie Clay, and has been researched and implemented in many countries around the world, including New Zealand, Australia, England, and the USA, where it has been in operation for over 30 years (Holliman and Hurry 2013; Pinnell 1989; Watson and Askew 2009). It is a short-term intervention that provides tutoring to the lowest achieving children who struggle with reading and writing after their first year at school. Trained Reading Recovery teachers deliver teaching one-to-one in daily 30-min pullout sessions over the course of 12–20 weeks. The program is supplementary to mainstream classroom literacy instruction and aims to foster the development of reading and writing strategies by tailoring individualized lessons to each student's needs.

In order to check whether Reading Recovery is considered to be an evidence-based practice three of the major sources can be consulted, Hattie's (2009) book, the Best Evidence Encyclopedia, and the What Works Clearinghouse. Hattie, in his synthesis of research on interventions in education, found Reading Recovery to have an above-average impact on children's achievement levels, with an effect size of 0.5. The Best Evidence Encyclopedia includes Reading Recovery in the list of "Top-Rated" reading programs with "strong evidence of effectiveness." The What Works Clearinghouse reports that Reading Recovery has the highest overall effectiveness rating for general reading achievement of all the 26 beginning reading programs reviewed. It is therefore clear that Reading Recovery is an intervention with a very strong base in research evidence and is therefore considered to be an evidence-based practice. So it is likely to be effective in the education systems in which it is used, as long as it is compatible with the practical reality of schools, available professional expertise, and relevant stakeholder perspectives, as discussed above.

Interventions That Are Not Evidence-Based Practices

In order for teaching to become a more evidence-based profession, in addition to identifying and implementing evidence-based practices, teachers need to be able to recognize and avoid interventions that are not evidence-based, including those that are not only ineffective but also potentially harmful (see Hornby et al. 1997;

Jacobson, Foxx & Mulick 2005; Pashler, McDaniel, Rohrer & Bjork 2009). To illustrate this distinction three examples of interventions that are not evidence-based practices and have been used in education for many years are outlined below.

Ability Grouping

As noted above, since Hattie found an effect size of 0.12 for ability grouping and the Teaching and Learning Toolkit reported that it is rated as having a negative impact based on moderate evidence, ability grouping is definitely not considered to be an evidence-based practice. However, many countries around the world continue to use different forms of ability grouping, such as streaming or setting, within education systems, between schools, within schools, or within classes. This continues despite extensive research evidence which shows that such ability grouping is at best ineffective and at worst harmful to students (Slavin 1987, 1990, 1993).

The worst form of ability grouping is when education systems use between-school grouping, with an examination to assess their "ability" at around 11 years of age to determine what level or type of school students will attend from then on. This between-school grouping is still used in many countries around the world and produces a high level of academic achievement for a minority of students at the expense of underachievement for the majority of students (Gorard & See 2013; Kutnick, Sebba, Blatchford, Galton, & Thorp 2005). In contrast, many countries use between-class ability grouping from around 11 years of age, with students assigned to classes designated as high, middle, and low ability. This practice is widespread despite schools acknowledging that there appears to be little benefit for most students and negative consequences, including low self-esteem and behavioral difficulties, for many students (Hornby & Witte 2014; Hornby, Witte & Mitchell 2011).

In their extensive review of the research literature on ability grouping Kutnick et al. (2005) concluded that no form of grouping benefits all students, but that students placed in lower ability groups are likely to make less progress, become demotivated, and develop anti-school attitudes. These students typically experience poorer quality of teaching and a limited range of curricular opportunities, which is likely to impact their chances later in life. The reviewers concluded that within-class grouping is the least detrimental and most effective form of ability grouping.

In summarizing the findings of research that has examined the impact of between-class ability grouping and mixed-ability grouping on student learning at the elementary, middle, and high school levels, Slavin (1996) has provided the following recommendations: use mixed-ability groups for most subject areas; encourage students' identification with mixed-ability groups in order to promote acceptance of diversity; and use ability grouping only when it will increase the efficacy of instruction or provide more time for teaching on specific skills such as in using setting for reading, mathematics, or spelling instruction. However, this is typically not how ability grouping is used in schools in most parts of the world.

Learning Styles

The notion of "learning styles" first emerged in the 1970s when it was suggested that students prefer either visual, auditory, tactual, or kinesthetic ways of learning (Dunn & Dunn 1979). It remains an extremely popular concept in the mainstream media, education literature, and teaching profession (Landrum & Landrum 2016) even though the Teaching and Learning Toolkit reports low impact based on limited evidence. Also, in Hattie's latest online update, matching teaching to learning style has an effect size of 0.23, which is well below the average effect size of 0.4 he calculated for educational interventions overall, indicating that it is not an evidence-based practice.

The rationale for the importance of learning styles is that learners differ in how they prefer to process information. If individual preferences and strengths can be identified, teaching can be matched to these strengths and therefore be more effective in facilitating learning. However, there is no accepted model of learning styles. In fact, a recent review identified 71 different schemes with 13 major models of learning styles, and although some overlapping concepts were found there was little direct comparability between models (Coffield, Moseley, Hall & Ecclestone 2004).

There is a plethora of commercially available checklists and inventories for measuring learning styles. Still, there is a general lack of reliability of these measures, and therefore a lack of evidence for the underpinning construct of learning styles, focusing doubt on the validity of the concept itself (Landrum & Landrum 2016). In addition, there is extremely limited empirical support for the notion of tailoring instruction to supposed learning styles, suggesting that the idea of matching instruction to learning styles is not a useful one and definitely not evidence-based (Willingham, Hughes & Dobolyi 2015).

It has been suggested that the widespread focus on learning styles in schools is unjustified and a waste of resources (Pashler et al. 2009). There are also dangers in labeling students with particular types of learning style. Teachers may emphasize specific learning styles, oversimplifying the learning process and limiting the learning experiences that students are exposed to, thereby jeopardizing learning outcomes. In conclusion, Pashler et al. (2009, p. 117) state, "The contrast between the enormous popularity of the learning styles approach within education and the lack of credible evidence for its utility is, in our opinion, striking and disturbing."

Irlen Lenses

Another intervention that is popular in schools is the use of colored filters and lenses for children with reading difficulties. It has been suggested that the use of these makes reading easier for some students by counteracting the perceptual dysfunction referred to as scotopic sensitivity syndrome (Irlen 1994, 1997). The Irlen Institute in the USA and centers in England, New Zealand, and Australia assess and treat students with reading difficulties, especially dyslexics. Irlen has claimed that 50% of people with dyslexia have visual perceptual difficulties that affect their ability to read and write. These include visual resolution, photophobia, and eye strain, as well as span, depth, and sustainability of focus. Irlen contends that these perceptual dysfunctions are components of scotopic sensitivity syndrome (Irlen 1994, 1997). This is claimed to adversely affect students' ability to read as a result of sensitivity to certain light sources, luminance, intensity, wavelengths, and color contrasts. The Irlen Institute treats such conditions by prescribing spectacles with tinted lenses and colored overlays to place over students' work. Irlen considers overlays to be an intermediate step toward alleviating symptoms, whereas tinted lenses are seen as potentially more effective (see Hornby et al. 1997).

Although some individuals claim to be more comfortable when using the tinted lenses or overlays, research has not demonstrated any significant gains in reading. A recent extensive review of studies concluded that, "… the research conducted on tinted lenses has failed to demonstrate the efficacy of the practice" (Hyatt, Stephenson & Carter 2009, p. 329). Therefore, research into the effectiveness of tinted lenses has produced findings that are unconvincing (Mallins 2009). Some researchers believe that the positive findings found in some studies of tinted lens treatments are due to a placebo effect. Also, much of the research conducted to date on this topic suffers from lack of controls, self-selection of subjects, lack of proper screening for vision defects, confusing terminology, and a marked lack of reliable data (Mallins 2009). Although tinted lenses may seem to be a harmless treatment, they do require a substantial financial outlay by parents. Since this expense and the child's emotional and physical energy are wasted on an ineffective treatment, it is considered that this approach should be avoided (Hyatt et al. 2009).

Key Evidence-Based Practices for Education

A review and analysis of the major sources of evidence-based practice, the Best Evidence Encyclopedia, the What Works Clearinghouse, the Teaching and Learning Toolkit, and Hattie's (2009) syntheses of meta-analyses, have revealed that there is a consistent consensus for the effectiveness of eight interventions that teachers can directly implement. It is therefore proposed that these eight interventions are key evidence-based strategies for improving student outcomes and that teachers at all levels of the education system would benefit from learning how to use them effectively. They are *teacher-student rapport, cooperative learning, peer tutoring, direct instruction, metacognitive strategies, formative assessment, functional behavioral analysis, and parental engagement.* The eight key evidence-based strategies are presented in Fig. 1.2.

The following chapters provide brief accounts of the theoretical and research evidence bases for the eight key evidence-based strategies. Examples of their implementation in early childhood, elementary school, and high school settings are included to provide guidelines for their use. For each of the eight key

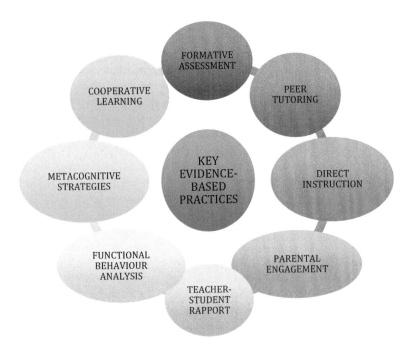

Fig. 1.2 Key evidence-based practices

evidence-based strategies, links are provided to brief videos of the strategies being used by teachers in classrooms in early childhood, elementary school, and high school classrooms from various countries around the world. It is intended that seeing the strategies in action in real-life settings will assist teachers in implementing these in their own classrooms and encouraging them to help their colleagues to do the same.

Although separate chapters are presented for each of the eight strategies it needs to be acknowledged that there are overlaps and links between each strategy and at least one of the others. For example, an important component of cooperative learning is peer tutoring. Similarly, formative assessment is a key element of Direct Instruction. Teacher-student rapport underpins all the other strategies, so it is presented first. Apart from this, the order of the chapters does not convey any indication of the magnitude of their importance. For example, parent engagement is presented last but is considered to be as important as all the other strategies.

Readers of both the print and electronic versions of the book can access the videos by putting the exact title of the video, highlighted in the text of chapters in italics, or the URLs of videos provided in the reference lists at the end of chapters, into their computer's internet browser (e.g., Safari) and conducting a google search to locate the video.

Conclusion

The rationale for this book is that effective teaching and improved student outcomes will result when evidence-based teaching strategies are used more widely in classrooms. Eight key evidence-based teaching strategies are identified, and guidelines for their use are supplemented by providing links to videos and other available free online resources.

References

Biesta, G. J. J. (2010). Why 'what works' still won't work: From evidence-based education to value-based education. *Studies in Philosophy and Education, 29,* 491–503.

Brown, C. (2013). *Making evidence matter: A new perspective for evidence-informed policy making in education.* Institute of Education Press.

Burns, M. K., & Ysseldyke, J. E. (2009). Reported prevalence of evidence-based instructional practices in special education. *Journal of Special Education, 43*(1), 3–11.

Canney, C., & Byrne, A. (2006). Evaluating circle time as a support to social skills development – Reflections on a journey in school-based research. *British Journal of Special Education, 33*(1), 19–24.

Coffield, F., Moseley, D., Hall, E., & Ecclestone, K. (2004). *Learning styles and pedagogy in post-16 learning: A systematic and critical review.* Learning and Skills Research Centre & Dept. for Education and Skills.

Cook, B. G., & Cook, S. C. (2011). Unravelling evidence-based practices in special education. *Journal of Special Education, 47*(2), 71–82.

Cook, B. G., & Odom, S. L. (2013). Evidence-based practices and implementation science in special education. *Exceptional Children, 79*(2), 135–144.

Cook, B. G., Tankersley, M., & Landrum, T. J. (2016). Instructional practices with and without empirical validity: An introduction. In B. G. Cook, M. Tankersley, & T. J. Landrum (Eds.), *Instructional practices with and without empirical validity: Advances in learning and behavioral disabilities* (pp. 1–16). Emerald.

DeLozier, S. J., & Rhodes, M. G. (2017). Flipped classrooms: A review of key ideas and recommendations for practice. *Educational Psychology Review, 29,* 141–151.

Dunn, R. S., & Dunn, K. J. (1979). Learning styles/teaching styles: Should they and can they be matched? *Educational Leadership, 36,* 238–244.

Gorard, S., & See, B. H. (2013). *Overcoming disadvantage in education.* Routledge.

Gorard, S., See, B. H., & Siddiqui, N. (2017). *The trials of evidence-based education.* Routledge.

Green, C., Taylor, C., Buckley, S., & Hean, S. (2016). Beyond synthesis: Augmenting systematic review procedures with practical principles to optimize impact and uptake in educational policy and practice. *International Journal of Research & Method in Education, 39*(3), 329–344.

Habib, A., Densmore-James, S., & Macfarlane, S. (2013). Culturally and linguistically diverse students. *Preventing School Failure, 57*(3), 171–180.

Hammersley, M. (2013). *The myth of research-based policy and practice.* Sage.

Hattie, J. (2009). *Visible learning: A synthesis of over 800 meta-analyses relating to achievement.* Routledge.

Hattie, J., & Timperley, H. (2007). The power of feedback. *Review of Educational Research, 77*(1), 81–112.

Higgins, S., & Katsipataki, M. (2016). Communicating comparative findings from meta-analysis in educational research: Some examples and suggestions. *International Journal of Research & Method in Education, 39*(3), 237–254.

Holliman, A. J., & Hurry, J. (2013). The effects of Reading recovery on children's literacy progress and special educational needs status: A three-year follow-up study. *Educational Psychology, 33*(6), 719–733.

Hornby, G., Atkinson, M., & Howard, J. (1997). *Controversial issues in special education.* David Fulton.

Hornby, G., Gable, B., & Evans, B. (2013). Implementing evidence-based practice in education: International literature reviews, what they tell us and what they don't. *Preventing School Failure, 57*(3), 119–123.

Hornby, G., & Witte, C. (2014). Ability grouping in New Zealand high schools: Are practices evidence-based? *Preventing School Failure, 58*(2), 90–95.

Hornby, G., Witte, C., & Mitchell, D. (2011). Policies and practices of ability grouping in New Zealand intermediate schools. *Support for Learning, 26*(3), 92–96.

Hyatt, K. J., Stephenson, J., & Carter, M. (2009). A review of three controversial educational practices: Perceptual motor programmes, sensory integration, and tinted lenses. *Education and Treatment of Children, 32*(2), 313–342.

Irlen, H. (1994). Scotopic sensitivity/Irlen syndrome – Hypothesis and explanation of the syndrome. *Journal of Behavioural Optometry, 5*, 62–65.

Irlen, H. (1997). Reading problems and Irlen coloured lenses. *Dyslexia Review, 8*(3), 4–7.

Jacobson, J. W., Foxx, R. M., & Mulick, J. A. (Eds.). (2005). *Controversial Therapies for Developmental Disabilities: Fad, Fashion, and Science in Professional Practice.* Lawrence Erlbaum.

Kutnick, P., Sebba, J., Blatchford, P., Galton, M., & Thorp, J. (2005). *The effects of student grouping: Literature review. Research report 688.* DfES.

Landrum, T. J., & Landrum, K. M. (2016). Learning styles, learning preferences, and student choice: Implications for teaching. In B. G. Cook, M. Tankersley, & T. L. Landrum (Eds.), *Instructional practices with and without empirical validity advances in learning and Behavioural disabilities* (pp. 135–152). Emerald.

Mallins, C. (2009). *The use of coloured filters and lenses in the management of children with reading difficulties: A literature review.* Ministry of Health.

Marzano, R. J. (1998). *A theory-based meta-analysis of research on instruction.* Mid-continent Regional Educational Laboratory.

Pampaka, M., Williams, J., & Homer, M. (2016). Is the educational 'what works' agenda working? Critical methodological developments. *International Journal of Research & Method in Education, 39*(3), 329–344.

Pashler, H., McDaniel, M., Rohrer, D., & Bjork, R. (2009). Learning styles: Concepts and evidence. *Psychological Science in the Public Interest, 9*, 105–119.

Pinnell, G. S. (1989). Reading recovery: Helping at-risk children learn to read. *Elementary School Journal, 90*(2), 160–183.

Schlosser, R. W., & Sigafoos, J. (2008). Identifying 'evidence-based practice' versus 'empirically supported treatment'. *Evidence-Based Communication Assessment and Intervention, 2*(2), 61–62.

Simpson, A. (2017). The misdirection of public policy: Comparing and combining standardised effect sizes. *Journal of Education Policy, 32*(4), 450–466.

Slavin, R. E. (1987). Ability grouping and student achievement in elementary schools: A best-evidence synthesis. *Review of Educational Research, 57*, 347–350.

Slavin, R. E. (1990). Achievement effects of ability grouping in high schools: A best-evidence synthesis. *Review of Educational Research, 60*, 471–499.

Slavin, R. E. (1993). Ability grouping in the middle grades: Achievement effects and alternatives. *Elementary School Journal, 93*, 535–552.

Slavin, R. E. (1996). *Education for all: Contexts of learning.* Swets and Keitlinger.

Slavin, R. E. (2008). Evidence-based reform in education: What will it take? *European Educational Research Journal, 7*(1), 124–128.

Vande Harr, M. J., & St. Pierre, N. (2006). Major advances in nutrition: Relevance to the sustainability of the dairy industry. *Journal of Dairy Science, 89*, 1280–1291.

Watson, B., & Askew, B. (Eds.). (2009). *Boundless horizons: Marie Clay's search for the possible in children's literacy*. Pearson.

Willingham, D. T., Hughes, E. M., & Dobolyi, D. G. (2015). The scientific status of learning styles theories. *Teaching of Psychology, 42*, 266–271.

Chapter 2
Teacher-Student Rapport

Abstract A powerful approach to facilitating highly effective teacher-student relationships is a learner-centered approach, focusing on the quality of relationships teachers have with their students, based on empathy, respect, and genuineness. In order to communicate these qualities, teachers need to develop a range of interpersonal skills. They need to develop listening skills, including paraphrasing, passive listening, and active listening. They also need to develop assertion skills, such as providing constructive feedback, handling criticism and aggression, and problem-solving. In addition, they need to develop group leadership skills of reaction, interaction, and action required for teaching social and emotional learning programs. Guidelines for developing these skills are provided in this chapter.

Rationale

It is widely recognized that the relationships which teachers establish, with individual students and groups of students in classrooms, are a critical element in the effectiveness of their teaching and thereby of the quality of education that students receive. Hattie (2009) found that the effect size for teacher-student relationships was 0.72, which is well above the average effect size and confirms the importance of the rapport that teachers establish with their students. In *Hattie's 2015 online update* he reports effect sizes of 0.52 for teacher-student relationships, 0.75 for teacher clarity, and 0.9 for teacher credibility. This suggests that establishing positive and constructive relationships with students is a key evidence-based practice. The main elements of this, especially clarity and credibility, are an important focus for teachers.

The effect that teachers have on students' cognitive as well as social and emotional outcomes has been found to be strongly influenced by students' psychological responses to teachers' actions and behaviors (Brophy & Good 1986; Wubbels & Brekelmans 2005). Specific teacher interpersonal behaviors that have been found to be consistently related to improved student outcomes include clarity, feedback, effective classroom management, and clear communication of teacher expectations

(Den Brok, Brekelmans & Wubbels 2004). High-quality teacher-student relationships have been shown to promote children's social functioning; reduce behavior
problems; increase engagement in learning activities; and improve levels of academic achievement (Roorda et al. 2011).

A powerful approach to facilitating highly effective teacher-student relationships
is the learner-centered approach, developed by Carl Rogers (1979, 1980). This
focuses on the quality of relationships that teachers have with their students. It
emphasizes the variables of empathy (understanding), unconditional positive regard
(respect), and genuineness (authenticity), which, when embodied by teachers, promote significant learning in students. In his meta-analysis, Cornelius-White (2007)
found that these learner-centered teacher variables had well above-average associations with positive student outcomes, cognitive, affective, and behavioral.

Therefore, one way to build highly effective teacher-student relationships is for
teachers to embody the key attitudes noted by Rogers that are essential for facilitating constructive relationships: genuineness, respect, and empathy. They should be
genuine and come across as real people with their own feelings and concerns. They
should respect students' views and not be judgmental. They should be empathic in
their understanding by taking into account students' perspectives and behavior. The
video entitled, *Carl Rogers on Person-Centered Therapy Video (PsychotherapyNet
2012)*, shows Carl Rogers explaining the value of embodying these three key
attitudes.

To communicate genuineness, respect, and empathy and thereby develop an
effective rapport with students, teachers must implement a range of interpersonal
skills in their interactions with individual students and classroom groups. They need
to use listening skills, especially paraphrasing, passive listening, and active listening. They also need to develop skills that are sometimes referred to as assertion
skills, such as providing constructive feedback, handling criticism and aggression,
and problem-solving. In addition, they need to develop the group leadership skills
of reaction, interaction, and action required for teaching social and emotional learning programs. These listening skills, assertion skills, and group leadership skills are
outlined below, and discussed in more detail elsewhere (see Hornby 2014; Hornby,
Hall & Hall 2003).

By developing these skills, teachers will be able to use them in a wide range of
situations with students, in classrooms, lunchrooms, playgrounds, and corridors,
both in fleeting interactions and longer meetings with individuals, small groups, and
classroom groups. It is not that teachers will use the skills outlined below for counseling students. Rather, they will use these counseling skills, assertion skills, and
interpersonal skills to build and maintain constructive relationships in which they
are genuine, respectful, and empathic. This will lay the foundation for teachers to
demonstrate credibility, constructive feedback, effective classroom instruction and
behavior management, and clear communication of expectations, which, as noted
above, are key components of effective teacher-student rapport.

High-quality teacher-student rapport is a necessary foundation for effective
implementation of the evidence-based teaching strategies discussed in the following
chapters of this book. Highly effective teacher-student rapport is essential for

effective formative assessment and functional behavioral analysis and successful implementation of cooperative learning and peer tutoring. It is useful when introducing students to metacognitive strategies and when implementing direct instruction. It is also essential to work effectively with parents, for example, in student-led parent-teacher conferences. So, overall, teacher-student rapport, based on the use of counseling skills, assertion skills, and interpersonal skills to communicate genuineness, respect, and empathy, is critical to optimizing student academic and social outcomes.

Listening Skills

The skills required for effective listening are outlined first as these are of prime importance and are the ones that are underpinned by the work of Carl Rogers, who emphasized the importance of empathic understanding, genuineness, and respect in developing facilitative relationships with others, including students, as noted above. The key components of listening skills, attentiveness, passive listening, paraphrasing, and active listening are outlined below.

Attentiveness

Effective listening requires a high level of attentiveness. This involves focusing one's physical attention on the person being listened to and includes several aspects outlined below.

Eye Contact: The importance for the listener of maintaining good eye contact throughout the interview cannot be overemphasized.

Facing Squarely: To communicate attentiveness, the listener needs to face the other person squarely or at a slight angle.

Leaning Forward: Leaning slightly forward toward the person being listened to communicates attentiveness.

Open Posture: Attentiveness is best communicated by adopting an open posture with both arms and legs uncrossed.

Remaining Relaxed: It is essential to be relaxed while adopting an attentive posture. If the posture adopted is uncomfortable, it is difficult to concentrate fully on what is being said.

Appropriate Body Motion: It is important to avoid distracting movements such as looking at the clock, fiddling with a pen, or constantly changing positions.

Non-distracting Environment: The room used should be as quiet as possible with the door kept closed and cell phones turned off to avoid distractions.

Distance: There needs to be a comfortable distance between the speaker and listener.

Passive Listening

Passive listening involves using a high level of attentiveness combined with other skills outlined below.

Invitations to Talk: Before beginning to listen, teachers need to extend an invitation to students to talk about their concerns. For example, "You seem unhappy today. Would you like to talk about it?"

Nonverbal Clues: Various "nonverbal clues" are used to let students know that you are paying attention to them without interrupting the flow, for example, "Go on," "Huh Huh," and "Mm Mm."

Open Questions: Open questions are used to encourage students to continue talking: for example, "How do you mean?" or "What happened then?" or "Tell me more about that."

Attentive Silence: Teachers should pause for a few seconds after each thing is said to allow students to say more if they want to.

Avoiding Communication Blocks: Certain comments tend to act as blocks to the communication process and should be avoided (Gordon 1970). When used, they stop students from exploring their concerns. A common example is *reassurance*, such as saying "Don't worry, I am sure it will work out alright." Other types of blocks are *denial* or *false acknowledgment of feelings*, such as suggesting that students should "Look on the bright side." Other common blocks involve *diverting* students from the topic, either directly or by the use of *excessive questioning* or by *excessive self-disclosure* when teachers talk too much about themselves or others they know who have had similar problems. More blatant blocks to communication are *criticism, sarcasm,* and *giving advice.* Further blocks involve *moralizing, ordering,* or *threatening*, that is, telling students what they ought to do. Finally, there are the blocks in which *diagnosis* or *labeling* is used, for example, telling students that they are "worriers." All these blocks to communication tend to stifle the exploration of concerns and are therefore best avoided.

Avoiding Self-Listening: Self-listening occurs when people drift off into their thoughts rather than listen to what others are saying. When a teacher is listening to a student and begins to self-listen, important aspects of what is said will be missed. The teacher may then become confused and unable to respond effectively to the student, who will therefore become aware of the inadequacy of the listening and tend to clam up. Therefore, it is very important that when teachers listen to students, they can reduce self-listening to a minimum. They can do this by using the listening techniques discussed below.

Paraphrasing

Paraphrasing is used when the main points of a message are fed back for confirmation. An effective paraphrase has four components. *First,* the paraphrase feeds back only the key points of what the student is saying. *Second,* paraphrasing is concerned with the factual content of the student's message, not with feelings. *Third,* an effective paraphrase is short and to the point. It is a summary of the student's key message, not a summary of everything said. *Fourth,* a paraphrase is stated in the teacher's own words and in language familiar to the student.

Paraphrases are used during natural breaks in the interaction, such as when the student pauses and looks to the teacher for a reaction, clearly wanting a response. The teacher needs to directly give feedback on the essence of the student's message and then wait for a response. When the paraphrase resonates with the student, they typically indicate this by saying "That's it" or "Yes" or by a nonverbal signal (nodding their head). If the paraphrase is not accurate, or only partly accurate, then the response will not be so positive, and the student may correct the listener. In so doing, students will clarify for themselves and the teacher exactly what they mean, so the paraphrase will still have value.

The video entitled *Paraphrasing & the PHI Coaching Approach to Communication* (PHInational 2011) presents a situation in which two adults are interacting with and without paraphrasing to demonstrate its use and effect on their communication and relationship.

Active Listening

Active listening involves trying to understand what the student is feeling and what the key message is in what they are saying, then putting this understanding into your own words, and feeding it back to them (Gordon 1970). Thus, active listening involves teachers actively engaging in clarifying the thoughts and feelings of the student to whom they listen. It builds on attentiveness, passive listening, and paraphrasing in that the main aspects of what is being communicated are reflected to the student. This is done to facilitate exploration and clarification of the student's concerns and feelings.

The process of active listening involves reflecting both thoughts and feelings to the student so that their specific feelings and reasons for those feelings are played back to them. When learning how to use active listening, it is useful to have a set formula to follow. The formula *"You feel .... because ...."* is typically used: for example: "You *feel* frustrated *because* you haven't finished the job." or "You *feel* delighted *because* you have done so well." When teachers gain confidence in their use of active listening, the formula is no longer needed and thoughts and feelings can be reflected more naturally: for example: "You *are* angry *about* how you were treated." and "You *are* pleased *with* the result."

Active listening requires teachers to set aside their views in order to understand what the student is experiencing. It, therefore, involves being aware of how things are said, the expressions and gestures used, and, most importantly, hearing what is not said but which lies behind what is said. The real art in active listening is in feeding this awareness back to the student accurately and sensitively. This is very difficult, but the feedback does not have to be entirely right all the time to be helpful. An active listening response that is a little off the mark typically gets students to clarify their thoughts and feelings further. An example of active listening is illustrated in a video from a popular TV show *Everybody Loves Raymond Uses Active Listening* (Parent Effectiveness 2013).

Assertion Skills

Assertiveness involves being able to stand up for one's own rights while respecting the rights of others and being able to communicate one's ideas, concerns, and needs directly, persistently, and diplomatically. It also involves being able to express both positive and negative feelings with openness and honesty and choose how to react to situations from a range of options (Bolton 1979). Teachers must deal with criticism or aggression from time to time and give constructive feedback, as well as help students to solve problems. The skills involved in these situations are outlined below and the rationale for assertiveness is presented in the video entitled *How to be Assertive* (Mindtools 2017).

Basic Elements of Assertiveness

Three aspects of assertiveness apply in any interaction teachers have with students or others: physical assertiveness, vocal assertiveness, and assertion muscle levels (Manthei 1981).

Physical Assertiveness

Assertive body language is a key component of effective assertion. The components of physical assertiveness are similar to those of the attentiveness required for effective listening. These include an open posture, facing the other person squarely, standing or sitting erect or leaning slightly forward, maintaining good eye contact, and not fidgeting or using superfluous gestures. What is different about assertiveness is that your facial expression matches the message's seriousness, and your feet are firmly planted on the floor when sitting or you are standing tall when delivering the message.

Vocal Assertiveness

To optimize the effectiveness of the message, it is helpful if your voice is firm but calm. It is best to speak a little more slowly than usual but at a normal volume and breathe deeply as this will help ensure enough breath to speak firmly and maintain calm.

Assertion Muscle Levels

Whenever being assertive, it is important to select the appropriate strength or "muscle level" of the assertive response used. Usually, it is best to start at the lowest muscle level or assertion strength, which is likely to achieve success. For example, "I would appreciate it if you could …." If this doesn't work, the muscle level is increased and the request repeated. For example, "It is important that you …." Muscle levels are then progressively increased until a satisfactory response is obtained: for example, from "It is essential that you …." to finally "I insist that you …."

   While verbal muscle levels are being increased, physical and vocal assertiveness can also be gradually made more intense, that is, by using a more serious facial expression and a firmer tone of voice with each increase in muscle level.

Giving Constructive Feedback

Constructive feedback aims to provide information to enable students to function better, so it is an essential skill for teachers to learn and use. A model for providing beneficial and constructive feedback is the DESC script, which stands for Describe, Express (and/or Explain), Specify, and Consequences (from Bower & Bower 1976). It is a technique that is particularly valuable in giving feedback to students whose behavior is difficult or challenging. The four steps involved in using the DESC script are described below.

Describe

Describe the behavior of concern in the most specific and objective terms possible. For example, *"When you shout out in class in response to my questions without putting your hand up …."*

Express and/or Explain

Either express your feelings about this behavior or explain the difficulties it causes for you, or do both, calmly and positively, without blaming or judging the other person or "putting them down." For example, *"… I get annoyed (*express*) because it disrupts the class (*explain*)."*

Specify

Specify the exact change in behavior you would like from the other student. For example, *"… so, in future, I would like you to put your hand up instead of shouting out …."*

Consequences

The consequences that are likely to result from the student complying with the request are stated. The benefits for both people involved are stated first, and then benefits for others. For example, *"… then, I will be happy to hear what you have to say, and the class will not be disturbed."*

If the student appears unwilling to comply, then the DESC script can be repeated at progressively higher muscle levels, specifying the negative consequences of non-compliance. For example, *"… if you continue to shout out rather than put your hand up, I will have to put you on detention …."*

Preparation and Delivery

Although the DESC script is often simple enough to be thought up and delivered on the spot, it is sometimes best to write it out beforehand. It is then possible to make sure that the wording is the most appropriate. It may also be helpful to rehearse it with a third person to get feedback on your draft. It can then be decided when, where, and how it can best be delivered.

The video entitled *Assertive Communication for Better Relationships: Train yourself to communicate what you need to* (Killam 2013) first distinguishes between aggression and assertion, and then explains each of the steps in the DESC script. Finally, it presents the CARE script as a valuable alternative strategy, similar to the DESC script.

Responding to Criticism

In dealing with criticism from students or others, it is important to consider the intention of the criticizer and any constructive suggestions for change. The four steps of a useful model for responding to criticism are outlined below (from Holland & Ward 1990).

Step One: Listening to the Criticism

Listening skills are useful in clarifying the criticism. Open questions such as "How do you mean?" or "Can you be more specific?" help determine exactly what the criticism aims at.

Step Two: Deciding on the Truth

Before responding to the criticism, its validity should be considered. It may be completely true, partly true, or completely untrue. One's assessment of the validity of the criticism will determine the response used in step three.

Step Three: Responding Assertively

If teachers consider the criticism to be entirely valid, it is best to apologize and say you will correct the situation. For example, "I'm sorry for not asking you about this. I'll make sure it doesn't happen again."

If the criticism is only partly true, then it is best to agree with the part considered to be valid, briefly apologize, and at the same time correct the false part. For example, "Yes, I did make a mistake in that case and I regret that, but I don't accept that I'm making mistakes all the time these days. I make occasional mistakes like anyone else."

Suppose teachers consider the criticism to be false. In that case, they should clearly reject it, tell the other person how the criticism makes them feel, ask for an explanation, and make an affirmative statement about themselves. For example, "I don't agree that I was wrong in that case and am annoyed by the suggestion. What grounds do you have for making that comment? My relationships with students are generally excellent."

Step Four: Letting Go

It is important to decide to use what you have learned from the criticism and about the criticizer and not be deflected by just one person's opinion.

Dealing with Aggression

In responding to aggressive behavior from students, teachers decrease their effectiveness when they argue with a student who is behaving aggressively; raise their voices or begin to shout; become defensive; or attempt to minimize the concern being expressed (Kroth 1985). These responses are commonly used by people confronted with aggression, but they often inflame the situation and make students even more aggressive. Teachers increase their effectiveness when, in dealing with aggression, they actively listen to the student, as explained above; speak softly, slowly, and calmly; ask for clarification of any vague complaints; ask what else is bothering students; make a list of their concerns, go through the list, and ask if it's correct; and use the technique of problem-solving, discussed below, to work through the list of concerns to resolve problems starting with the one of the highest priority.

Problem-Solving

The following six-step model for solving problems, proposed by Bolton (1979), is helpful to teachers for solving issues with individual students and can be taught to whole classes so that students can learn and use this technique for themselves at school and beyond. The six steps are as follows:

1. *Define Problem in Terms of the Needs of Each Person*
   This involves the use of active listening to clarify the other person's needs and, if possible, to understand the reason for these needs. It also involves stating one's own needs assertively. This is a key element of the model and may take up to half of the total time required for the process.
2. *Brainstorming Possible Solutions*
   Once both persons' needs are understood, brainstorming can seek solutions that meet both sets of needs. First, as many potential solutions as possible should be listed, without evaluating or clarifying any of them. Then, each other's ideas should be expanded on and clarified.
3. *Evaluate and Select a Solution That Best Meets Both Parties' Needs*
   A choice is then made from the list of potential solutions that best meet the needs of both parties. This will probably involve discussing the relative merits of several solutions in meeting each other's needs.
4. *Plan Who Will Do What, Where, and by When*
   It is useful to make a written note of what each party will do, where they will do it, and when it will be completed.
5. *Implement the Plan*
   Each party must attempt to follow the agreement precisely in implementing the plan.
6. *Review and Evaluate the Process and the Solution*
   An essential part of the problem-solving process is to agree on a time when both parties can meet to evaluate how well the solution meets each of their needs and discuss possible changes to the plan to improve the situation.

The brief video entitled *5 Step Problem Solving Process* (Darrow 2016), presents a similar method to that above, with some valuable tips for its use. In this five-step sequence, steps four and five of the above model are combined.

Teaching Programs of Social and Emotional Development

Teachers have an essential role in facilitating their students' social and emotional well-being and fostering positive mental health. They can do this through teaching programs for promoting students' social and emotional learning and positive mental health (Lendrum, Humphrey and Wigelsworth 2013). A meta-analysis of 213 school-based social and emotional learning programs found that participating students demonstrated significantly improved social and emotional skills and academic achievement and significantly reduced behavioral problems and internalizing issues (Durlak et al. 2011). It also found that classroom teachers could effectively deliver these programs and that they were successful at all education levels from elementary through high schools and in urban, suburban, and rural settings.

Weare and Nind (2011) analyzed 52 systematic reviews and meta-analyses of interventions promoting positive mental health in schools. The interventions identified by the reviews had a wide range of beneficial effects on children, families, and communities and a range of mental health, social, emotional, and educational outcomes. The characteristics of more effective interventions included teaching specific skills and competencies, focusing on positive mental health, balancing school-wide and targeted approaches, and providing early and ongoing interventions. A key finding was the importance of embedding interventions within a whole-of-school approach, which included changes to the curriculum, linking with academic learning, improving school ethos, working with parents and outside agencies, and developing teachers' skills.

Therefore, teachers must develop the skills to teach programs to promote social and emotional aspects of students" development. These programs need to be well established, used in a wide range of settings, and have solid research evidence for their effectiveness. The two approaches below meet these criteria and are compatible, so they can be implemented in the same school within a whole-of-school approach to promoting social and emotional development.

Circle Time

Circle Time is a model developed and popularized by Jenny Mosley in England in the 1980s (Mosley 1996) and has been adapted and widely used in schools in many countries. Circle Time is generally conducted as a class-wide procedure, with everyone sitting in a circle, hence the name. Circle Time has been used with children from preschool to secondary school ages. It is a straightforward approach for teachers to learn, particularly if specialist staff such as psychologists or counselors can help set it up and model several sessions to get them started (Kelly 1999).

The video clip, entitled *Jenny Mosley's Quality Circle Time The Five Skills* (Mosley 2015), presents Jenny demonstrating the five core condition skills underpinning Circle Time with a class of young children.

As well as teaching children social and emotional development skills the Circle Time model can be used to establish and maintain a positive behavior management system; promote positive relationships; create a caring and respectful ethos; help children develop their self-esteem and self-confidence; facilitate happy lunchtimes and playtimes; nurture the creativity in all children; and promote the social and emotional development of all children.

Research on Circle Time has reached a point where studies have now used randomized control trials and produced findings demonstrating its effectiveness, confirming that it is an evidence-based practice (Canney & Byrne 2006; Miller & Moran 2007).

Incredible Years Programs

The Incredible Years program includes training programs for teachers, psychologists, and therapists to promote children's social competence, emotional regulation, and problem-solving skills and reduce their behavior problems (Webster-Stratton & Reid 2010). The objectives of Incredible Years program interventions are to help teachers, along with parents, to provide young children of up to 12 years of age with a solid emotional, social, and academic foundation. The longer term goal is to enhance children's ability to become socially and emotionally competent individuals who succeed in school, thereby reducing the incidence of social and emotional problems such as depression, school dropouts, violence, drug abuse, and delinquency in later years.

Incredible Years programs have been developed and evaluated by Carolyn Webster-Stratton in the USA during the past 30 years and are used in over 20 countries worldwide. Numerous randomized control group studies have been conducted to evaluate the effectiveness of Incredible Years Teacher, Parent, and Child intervention programs for promoting social and emotional competence. These studies have consistently reported positive findings, so these programs are considered to be evidence-based practices (Fergusson, Horwood & Stanley 2013; Webster-Stratton & Reid 2010). The video entitled *The Incredible Years Overview* (The Incredible Years 2013a) provides the rationale for and overview of the available series of programs.

The Incredible Years Program Series has linked comprehensive and developmentally based programs targeting teachers, parents, and children. The programs work jointly to promote emotional, social, and academic competence and prevent, reduce, and treat behavioral and emotional problems in young children.

The Incredible Years program for teachers focuses on helping them strengthen classroom management strategies, promoting children's pro-social behavior, and reducing classroom disruption and aggression. The program is helpful for teachers, teacher aides, psychologists, school counselors, and any school personnel working with young children.

The Incredible Years program for children focuses on strengthening children's social, emotional, and academic competencies, including understanding and communicating feelings, using effective problem-solving strategies, managing anger, learning conversational skills, and appropriate classroom behaviors. Teachers can use the Incredible Years Program for Children training course as a prevention program with entire classes of students. An example of a widely used program is presented in the video entitled *Content of The Incredible Years Dinosaur School Child Training Program* (The Incredible Years 2013b).

Teacher Skills for Leading Social and Emotional Learning Programs

The key skills needed to lead social and emotional learning (SEL) with students are the listening skills outlined earlier in this chapter. However, teachers also need to be able to use group leadership skills to develop trust within the student group and maintain a focus on program goals. Further, teachers need to be responsive to what is happening within the student group, and they need to be perceived by students as being with them as a group and for them as individuals (Dinkmeyer & Muro 1979). Therefore, teachers need to develop the group leadership skills of reaction, interaction, and action, as suggested by Trotzer (1977), that are briefly outlined below and discussed at more length in Hornby (2011) and Hornby et al. (2003).

The *reaction skills* which teachers need in order to lead SEL programs are:

- *Listening*: in order to communicate respect, acceptance, empathy, and caring
- *Restating*: to convey to students that they are being heard
- *Reflecting*: in order to convey understanding and help students to express themselves
- *Clarifying*: in order to better understand confusing aspects of what is said
- *Summarizing*: to provide an overview, stimulate reactions and move on to new ground

The *interaction skills* which teachers need to lead SEL programs are:

- *Moderating*: to ensure that all students have the opportunity to talk
- *Interpreting*: to help students gain insight into what is happening within the group
- *Linking*: to tie together common elements within the group and promote cohesiveness
- *Blocking*: to prevent undesirable comments or actions by one or more students
- *Supporting*: to encourage students to share of themselves safely within the group
- *Limiting*: to prevent actions which would infringe the rights of any student in the group
- *Protecting*: to prevent students from being unduly criticized or hurt.
- *Consensus taking*: to help students see where they stand relative to others

The *action skills* which teachers need to lead SEL programs are:

- *Questioning*: to help students to consider aspects they had not thought of
- *Probing:* to help students to look more deeply into their concerns

- *Tone setting:* to establish an atmosphere and standards to be adhered to
- *Confronting:* to help students face things about themselves which they are avoiding
- *Personal sharing:* to show that the teacher is human and is prepared to be open
- *Modeling:* to teach students interpersonal skills such as active listening

Teachers need to use these reaction, interaction, and action skills in leading class-wide intervention strategies such as Circle Time and the Incredible Years social and emotional learning programs described above. These skills are also useful for leading many other interventions focused on promoting student mental health and well-being that enable the creation of a caring and respectful ethos in the classroom and help establish positive relationships with and between students and facilitate effective teacher-student rapport. These include the well-established and easy-to-implement approach of developmental group work (Allan & Nairne 1984) as well as newly developed interventions such as mindfulness training for children (Singh & Singh Joy 2021), both of which do not yet have adequate research evidence to be considered evidence-based practices but are very promising approaches.

Conclusion

The interpersonal skills needed for facilitating highly effective teacher-student relationships based on empathy, respect, and genuineness were highlighted in this chapter. The importance of teachers developing listening skills, assertion skills, and group leadership skills in order to communicate these qualities was emphasized, and guidelines for their use were provided. The skills discussed in this chapter underpin the high quality of rapport needed with students to effectively utilize the evidence-based teaching strategies presented in the following chapters.

References

Allan, J. A. B., & Nairne, J. (1984). *Class discussions for teachers and counsellors in the elementary school.* Faculty of Education, University of Toronto.

Bolton, R. (1979). *People skills.* Prentice-Hall.

Bower, S. A., & Bower, G. H. (1976). *Asserting yourself.* Addison-Wesley.

Brophy, J. E., & Good, T. L. (1986). Teacher behavior and student achievement. In M. C. Wittrock (Ed.), *Handbook of research on teaching* (3rd ed., pp. 328–375). Macmillan.

Canney, C., & Byrne, A. (2006). Evaluating circle time as a support to social skills development – Reflections on a journey in school-based research. *British Journal of Special Education, 33*(1), 19–24.

Cornelius-White, J. (2007). Learner-centred teacher-student relationships are effective: A meta-analysis. *Review of Educational Research, 77*(1), 113–143.

Darrow, D. (2016, February 27). *5 Step problem solving process [Video].* YouTube. https://www.youtube.com/watch?v=foBaDnywUxk

Den Brok, P., Brekelmans, M., & Wubbels, T. (2004). Interpersonal teacher behaviour and student outcomes. *School Effectiveness and School Improvement, 15*(3-4), 407–442.

Dinkmeyer, D. C., & Muro, J. J. (1979). *Group counselling: Theory and practice* (2nd ed.). Peacock.

Durlak, J. A., Weissberg, R. P., Dymnicki, A. B., Taylor, R. D., & Schellinger, K. B. (2011). The impact of enhancing students' social and emotional learning: A meta-analysis of school-based universal interventions. *Child Development, 82*(1), 405–432.

Fergusson, D. M., Horwood, L. J., & Stanley, L. (2013). A preliminary evaluation of the incredible years teacher programme. *New Zealand Journal of Psychology, 42*(2), 51–56.

Gordon, T. (1970). *Parent effectiveness training*. Wyden.

Hattie, J. (2009). *Visible learning: A synthesis of over 800 meta-analyses relating to achievement*. Routledge.

Holland, S., & Ward, C. (1990). *Assertiveness: A practical approach*. Winslow Press.

Hornby, G. (2011). *Parental involvement in childhood education: Building effective school-family partnerships*. Springer.

Hornby, G. (2014). *Inclusive special education: Evidence-based practices for children with special needs and disabilities*. Springer.

Hornby, G., Hall, E., & Hall, C. (Eds.). (2003). *Counselling pupils in schools: Skills and strategies for teachers*. Routledge Falmer.

Kelly, B. (1999). Circle time. *Educational Psychology in Practice, 15*(1), 40–44.

Killam, L. (2013, January 29). *Assertive communication for better relationships: Train yourself to communicate what you need to [Video]*. YouTube. https://www.youtube.com/watch?v=BHk_S54ZAH8

Kroth, R. L. (1985). *Communicating with parents of exceptional children* (2nd ed.). Love.

Lendrum, A., Humphrey, N., & Wigelsworth, M. (2013). Social and emotional aspects of learning (SEAL) for secondary schools: Implementation difficulties and their implications for school-based mental health promotion. *Child and Adolescent Mental Health, 18*(3), 158–164.

Manthei, M. (1981). *Positively me: A guide to assertive behaviour*. Methuen.

Miller, D., & Moran, T. (2007). Theory and practice in self-esteem enhancement: Circle time and efficacy-based approaches—A controlled evaluation. *Teachers and Teaching: Theory and Practice, 13*(6), 601–615.

Mindtools. (2017, October 13). *How to be assertive [Video]*. YouTube. https://www.youtube.com/watch?v=lrUmTRAlBFg

Mosley, J. (1996). *Quality circle time in the primary classroom: Our essential guide to enhancing self-esteem, self-discipline and positive relationships*. LDA.

Mosley, J. (2015, August 4). *Jenny Mosley's quality circle time the five skills [Video]*. YouTube. https://www.youtube.com/watch?v=ZXOi4nrR4hM

Parent Effectiveness. (2013, February 21). *Everybody loves Raymond uses active listening – from Parent effectiveness training [Video]*. YouTube. https://www.youtube.com/watch?v=4VOubVB4CTU

PHInational. (2011, June 22). *Paraphrasing & the PHI coaching approach to communication [Video]*. YouTube. https://www.youtube.com/watch?v=QRfTylX46pU

PsychotherapyNet. (2012, November 14). *Carl Rogers on person-centered therapy video [Video]*. YouTube. https://www.youtube.com/watch?v=o0neRQzudzw

Rogers, C. R. (1979). *Freedom to learn*. Merrill.

Rogers, C. R. (1980). *A way of being*. Houghton Mifflin.

Roorda, D. L., Kooman, H. M. Y., Spilt, J. L., & Oort, F. J. (2011). The influence of affective teacher-student relationships on students' school engagement and achievement: A meta-analytic approach. *Review of Educational Research, 81*(4), 493–529.

Singh, N. N., & Singh Joy, S. D. (2021). *Mindfulness-based interventions with children and adolescents: Research and practice*. Routledge.

The Incredible Years. (2013a, July 5). *The incredible years overview [Video]*. YouTube. https://www.youtube.com/watch?v=liRCsK7YmY8

The Incredible Years. (2013b, December 13). *Content of The Incredible Years® dinosaur school child training program [Video]*. YouTube. https://www.youtube.com/watch?v=73zYE-FDnIs

Trotzer, J. P. (1977). *The counselor and the group*. Brooks/Cole.

Weare, K., & Nind, M. (2011). Mental health promotion and problem prevention in schools: What does the evidence say? *Health Promotion International, 26*(S1), i29–i69.

Webster-Stratton, C., & Reid, M. J. (2010). The incredible years parents, teachers, and children training series: A multifaceted treatment approach for young children with conduct disorders. In J. R. Weisz & A. E. Kazdin (Eds.), *Evidence-based psychotherapies for children and adolescents* (2nd ed.). Guilford.

Wubbels, T., & Brekelmans, M. (2005). Two decades of research on teacher-student relationships in class. *International Journal of Educational Research, 43*(1-2), 6–24.

Chapter 3
Formative Assessment

Abstract The content explored in this chapter advances the premise that ongoing formative assessment of student work, in conjunction with frequent feedback, is critical to helping teachers monitor learning progress and adapt their instruction to meet student needs. Formative assessment is an approach that uses careful planning for assessment to include various instruments beyond just pencil and paper. Information gathered through assessments is discussed in terms of its value toward goal setting for students and teachers.

Rationale

Traditionally, most assessments in schools have been summative assessments used to measure the knowledge and skills that students have acquired over time. Examples of such assessments include evaluations of student performance at the end of a week, end of the term, end of a semester, or end of a school year. Typically, these evaluations identify where students are performing at the end of a predetermined learning cycle. In comparison, formative assessment concerns itself with evaluating the learning that occurs within a shorter cycle. For all students, especially those who experience learning challenges, teachers' knowledge about performance during actual instruction is a critical planning tool. Formative assessment differs from other forms of assessment in that the focus is on where the student currently is, where they are going, and how they are going to get there (Wiliam 2017). On the international front, reviews of teacher accountability practices across continents increasingly include teachers' practical use of formative assessment to drive instructional practices (Darling-Hammond 2017).

Formative assessment typically involves gathering evidence through a variety of student products. With formative assessment, student work products provide the substance for reflective feedback. Feedback to students and teachers is a critical aspect of formative assessment. It is through feedback that appropriate modifications to learning are identified and implemented. The *Teaching and Learning Toolkit* (Education Endowment Foundation 2021) reports that feedback has a very high impact for very low cost based on extensive evidence. This suggests that by exposing students to more systematic and meaningful assessment methods, including feedback, they become more adept at self-monitoring and regulating their learning. The idea is to maximize formative assessment efforts to prompt further teaching and guide learning steps during the instructional cycle. Based on Hattie's (2009) meta-analyses of the impact of the components of formative assessment, feedback involving cues and reinforcement has been found to have an average effect size of 0.92 (*Hattie's online synthesis of meta-analyses*). Also, formative assessment overall has been found to result in an average effect size of 0.90 (Hattie 2009; Hattie & Zierer 2018). These are well above average effect sizes, which confirm that formative assessment that incorporates feedback is an invaluable aspect of the teaching process and an evidence-based practice. Its principal value is helping teachers and their students identify and process what and how learning occurs while teaching and learning experiences are underway. In this way, teachers can pinpoint content areas and specific students that need additional attention or extension. Formative assessment provides valuable information about how students respond to and demonstrate their understanding of the various learning tasks they are undertaking. Formative assessments involve frequent student-centered information-gathering events that consider students' current performance levels, interests, and preferences. These types of information help guide teachers toward more targeted teaching and learning (Tomlinson & Moon 2013).

The video, *What formative assessment is and isn't* (Wiliam 2020a), is a powerful introduction to formative assessment by Dylan Wiliam, who has spent much of his career in education focusing on formative assessment and the critical importance of providing students with feedback.

Theory

The vast amount of research to determine effective evidence-based strategies has demonstrated strong associations between formative assessment and improved student achievement (Hattie 2009). Assessing the current state of students' knowledge and skills to facilitate future learning can be conducted in a short cycle, which occurs between lessons, or longer cycles occurring between instructional units (Kluthe et al. 2017). The key to effective intervention is to provide timely feedback to teachers to help them adapt instructional content and methodology.

The most useful formative assessment provides both student-directed and other-directed feedback (Black & Wiliam 2009). Formative assessment focuses on students by incorporating tools and actions to appraise or monitor their work, performance, strategies, and progress. Reviews that are student focused allow students to think and reflect on their performance and work products and help them to determine their next steps. However, formative assessment also focuses on appraising and monitoring the teachers' work; the utility of various teacher tools, including computer assessment programs; the strategies used; students' work performance; and students' overall progress and learning interaction.

Effective use of formative assessment to improve students' performance is an ongoing process. The process includes setting lesson intentions or goals, gathering evidence about student learning, and providing feedback for actions needed for students to clarify and improve their performance (Hattie & Timperley 2007).

Performance Feedback

Feedback involves developing and communicating thoughts, ideas, and recommendations about what has occurred and what is apparent or unclear. Among other possibilities, feedback delivery may include verbal review, discussion, reflection, and sharing, as well as written comments. When formative assessments provide timely and meaningful feedback, teachers can better reflect on and adjust their actions and heighten students' awareness of their actions while engaged in the learning process (Hattie 2012). Thus, formative assessment is a critical tool that should be added to a teacher's repertoire and incorporated into their lesson plans. Teachers must create the time to analyze and assess needs based on evidence gained from formative assessment. Information gathered by looking over students' work products and observing their work habits provides valuable insight into performance. The results of formative assessments can serve as a compass to identify strengths and gaps in student learning. Teachers can use these insights to develop helpful feedback with their students and simultaneously evaluate their teaching practices.

As teachers work with students to guide them toward learning targets and provide opportunities to practice and demonstrate their learning, it is imperative to involve students in a learning cycle where they receive input and opportunities to reflect on their practices and actions. Taking time to reflect on the completion of work and the accomplishment it represents is enhanced when feedback becomes a part of the assessment cycle.

Providing opportunities for feedback to students can have a significant influence on their learning outcomes. However, the negative or positive feedback and the timing of the input are essential considerations. Hattie and Timperley (2007) recommend a model for feedback that focuses on answering three questions: "Where is the learner going?" "How is the learning going?" "Where does the learner need to go next?" Useful feedback focuses on sending explicit messages to students about what they need to do differently and how they can most effectively and accurately move forward with the assignment toward accurate completion.

In the video, *Feedback for moving students forward*, Wiliam (2020b) notes that feedback specific to directly supporting students' work provides more significant gains. Feedback consisting of only scores, or feedback associated with students' ego or emotions, such as nonspecific praise, is less helpful. The most effective feedback encourages students to reflect on their work and provides them with guidance on improving.

Formative Assessment Practices

Planning

Given the theoretical considerations mentioned so far, teachers should carefully prepare their formative assessment strategy to include all the necessary components. They should start each lesson with a clear plan for conducting assessments and anticipating the appropriate timing to use formative assessment before, during, or toward the lesson's end. Just as teachers typically plan lessons around content, method, and materials needed for their lesson delivery, and summative assessments, they should also prepare for the more immediate short-term formative assessments.

Teachers should establish how they will get evidence from and about students. If questioning is a method used to gather formative data, teachers can prepare several of the questions they may ask students and have a strategy for how and what short-term data they will collect. For instance, will expectations for responses be written or orally presented, or will drawing a picture be sufficient? They should plan how to respond quickly to gauge their students' processing and thinking and plan how they and their students will reflect on feedback to assess their performance to determine the next steps. The methods for determining which content and skills are appropriate for student-directed or other-directed formative assessment also need to be planned. These considerations warrant a thoughtful approach to lesson planning.

In later sections of this chapter, suggestions are made about implementing formative assessment strategies relatively quickly to provide current information. This information provides the evidence needed to diversify and differentiate instruction to address students' needs, including those experiencing challenges.

Frequency and Timing

Though actual classroom lesson times may vary across school systems in different countries, the traditional time frame in most primary through secondary school settings can span from 45 to 90 minutes. Whether conducted within a lesson or curriculum unit, and whether they are student-directed or other-centered, the goal of formative assessment is that they are frequent and timely. A timely occurrence allows for more immediate corrective feedback. Periodic assessments train the teacher and students to become more adept at monitoring their learning processes. When working with teachers to improve their skills using effective formative assessment strategies, Wiliam (2017) stresses the importance of activating students' skills to become adept at regulating their learning.

Using Formative Assessment Information

The value of formative assessments rests in their ability to help teachers and learners set goals for learning, to monitor the effectiveness of instruction and learning, and as a means of gathering meaningful data that can be analyzed and considered to guide corrective feedback. Identifying and strategizing the next steps for teacher instructions and actions needed by the learner are necessary to progress toward learning goals. Ultimately, formative assessments consider the work products and the processes involved in creating and reflecting on the product.

Setting Goals for Learning: Where Is the Learner Going?

Setting intentions or goals for the lesson is essential to establish the focus of the task. It starts to guide the thinking process toward the types of content, experiences, and current understanding students have on the topic. It also helps set up student expectations for the planned activities and how they are to be involved in the learning process. For example, an intention may be to depict or explain the cycle through which a caterpillar becomes a butterfly. Students may first observe a video or listen to a story and then verbally share what they saw and heard. Alternatively, they may be asked to sequence pictures to depict the cycle or create a visual chart to sequence and explain it. Setting intentions such as these focuses their thinking on the topic and prepares them for the activities. On occasion, especially with older students and more open-ended issues, it may help to set more general learning intentions. This approach is more appropriate for abstract content and situations where the goal is to encourage students to make correlations and generalizations (Marzano 2010; Wiliam 2017). Formative assessments at this stage may require students to set personal goals by identifying information they would like to learn and skills they would like to accomplish by the time the lesson or unit concludes. Alternately, they may be given a series of learning goals and asked to consider the extent to which their projects and assignments demonstrate the accomplishment of the provided goals.

Monitoring the Learner: Where Is the Learner Functioning Now?

Formative assessments can also serve a crucial role in monitoring students' work and performance before, during, and after the instructional process. These formative assessments provide insight into the learning process that a student may use to conduct and complete an assignment. The aim is to adopt inclusive practices by acknowledging that students have a range of knowledge and skills. Assessment methods must be sufficiently varied to gather insight into students' levels of understanding. Teachers can then determine appropriate teaching practices based on such information. For example, assessment information may suggest that a particular student with reading challenges needs to listen to reading passages as they follow along in a text before answering questions. For others, assessments may indicate that they require visuals and charts or would benefit more from three-dimensional representations of information to support their learning. In practice, plans for the formative evaluation using various projects and assignments will allow students to demonstrate what they are learning and help identify areas where different types of instruction are needed (Chapman & King 2012; Marzano, Pickering & Pollock 2001).

Integrating formative assessment as a routine feature of the instructional process, collecting, analyzing, and acting on the findings are central to teachers' efforts to improve student learning (Tomlinson 2014). At the core of formative assessment is the notion that whether students provide verbal responses, scripted responses on a post-it note, raised hands to signal agreement or disagreement, or a quickly sketched picture or diagram; all answers provide useable information to teachers. All these different methods engage students in producing a response that serves as evidence of their learning.

Practices That Support Formative Assessment

Several teaching practices illustrate the vision of formative assessment as a deliberate and ongoing process primarily concerned with the frequent and purposeful evaluation of students. Several of these practices are discussed below and should become everyday practices in classrooms. These practices include observing students as they work, asking questions to promote thinking, encouraging them to reflect on their work, and appropriately administering curriculum-based assessments.

Observation

Observation of students completing a learning task can be casual or may involve written documentation. Regardless of the method taken, observation data characterize students' and teachers' actions and their impact on learning when appropriately captured and reviewed. Observing work completion and behaviors during the instructional process is invaluable. As teachers walk around the classroom and watch, they gain insight into how students process information. Monitoring students as they demonstrate or explain their solutions to a partner or small group gives insight into the depth of their understanding. This type of information identifies gaps in knowledge and skills and sets the agenda for what needs to be retaught or extended.

Questioning

Asking questions may be one of the more common approaches teachers use to solicit information from students. However, how they use the responses to these questions is what matters most. Questions should be purposeful, aimed at engaging their interest and getting insight into the depth of their understanding (Black et al. 2004). The video, *Strategies for Monitoring Progress* (EL Education 2018), features a science lesson where the teacher engages students in creating cartoon strips to demonstrate the interconnection between the earth and other planets in the solar system. At the end of the lesson, the teacher collects data by questioning students and soliciting responses to determine the extent to which they believed they were meeting the intermediate goals associated with their assignments. Students reflect and chart their progress toward approaching, meeting, or exceeding their targets.

At the secondary school level, checking for understanding by asking probing questions is critical to gathering formative information. To increase effectiveness, teachers should use questions appropriate to the target of the learning intentions. Teachers should also start with more straightforward questions and gradually increase the levels of complexity. The following hierarchy of questions from Anderson and Krathwohl (2001) represents an adaptation from Bloom and Krathwohl's (1956) taxonomy. The framework for this hierarchy of questions is as follows:

Knowledge based: Questions that require recall of information.
Comprehension based: Questions that require restating or interpreting meaning.
Application based: Questions that require the application of ideas to new situations or problems.
Analysis based: Questions that require breaking down information or problems, to look for relationships.
Evaluation based: Questions that seek judgments based on available criteria.
Synthesis based: Questions that require responses that bring together different aspects of a situation to develop new or creative thinking.

Self-Reflection

Student-directed formative assessments encourage students to actively participate in activities that promote self-reflection and heighten their metacognitive awareness (see Chap. 7). Student-directed assessments engage students in looking at their work and reflecting on the extent to which they believe themselves to be reaching their learning targets. The use of rubrics and checklists, referenced later in this chapter, encourages self-reflection while also guiding actions and providing formative assessment.

The Australian Institute of Teaching and School Leadership (2017), in their video, *Formative assessment in the classroom*, demonstrates how teachers share formative assessment information with their students as they seek to involve them in the learning process. In these classroom vignettes, lessons are started with the teacher engaging students in conversation to clarify the day's learning intentions. Teachers use visual aids and charts to help their students identify and rate their performance. The video demonstrates the use of a "*Traffic Light*" self-assessment system from which students may rate their progress along a continuum of meeting their learning intentions for that day: "I can do it; I am nearly there; I am not sure yet." This example illustrates using simple teacher-created tools to provide feedback to adjust the focus of future lessons.

Criterion-Based Assessments

Other approaches to formative assessment collect data through more direct methods. These methods assess performance based on specific criteria relevant to skills, concepts, or content that students are taught. Assessments are often paper-and-pencil assessments or internet-based interactive programs. A benefit of using interactive internet programs is their ready access to response data. Such assessments, referred to as curriculum-based or criterion-referenced assessments, are diagnostic tools. They encourage teachers to reflect on the assessment information to identify students' strengths and challenges and decide what areas need to be readdressed to improve instructional effectiveness. Understanding the expectations of the curriculum and where students perform within those expectations is critical to effective teaching. Frequently teachers must navigate within guidelines set by their districts to gather formative data on their students. In their video, *Criterion Referenced Test & National Assessment*, The Barbados Government Information Service (2019), provides an example of how a school principal in Barbados directs teachers to administer criterion-referenced assessments to gather formative data on their students. Their intended goals are to determine what skills are mastered, identify learning deficits, and to formulate improvement plans.

Teachers can also effectively create tools for conducting a formative assessment by including everyday items into their arsenal. Such things may consist of post-it notes for recording responses or color-coded cards with associated choices such as agree/disagree/do not know. When the teacher provides a prompt or question to gauge understanding, students can respond readily. Whether formal or informal, the intent of these exercises is geared toward improving teaching practices and learning trends of the students.

Cooperative Learning Strategies

Cooperative learning strategies often provide opportunities for teachers to engage in formative assessment while the cooperative activity is underway. Two examples of such activities are *think-pair-share* and *four corners* which are described in detail in Chapter 5. During these types of activities, students are asked to share and discuss information or are required to select what they believe to be an appropriate answer, with opportunities to change their response when additional information is provided by the teacher or peers. Such opportunities allow a teacher to gather observational data and to listen to and evaluate responses while the activity is underway. This type of formative data helps determine corrective actions relevant to what reteaching and differentiation of content are needed. Frequently, this corrective action on the teacher's part can be taken within the context of the activity, thus addressing the students' needs in a timely manner.

Formative Assessment Strategies for Preschool and Elementary Students

Various early learning theorists such as Piaget, Erikson, Vygotsky, and Montessori share the fundamental understanding that most children in their early stages of learning, birth through school age, are developing and learning quickly (Mooney 2013). In their formative years, young learners absorb information and subsequently learn in response to new and changing stimuli that they receive. How students respond allows teachers to gather anecdotal observations and tangible products that help explain their actions.

Over the years, the authors' visits to early elementary settings reveal that adults constantly observe and react to students' actions throughout the day. These adults provide frequent verbal information, redirection, and correction. Feedback to students tends to be quick when related to behavior and sometimes longer in delivery when related to cognitive tasks. In considering formative assessment for younger students, teachers should take advantage of the fact that young children generally respond like "developmental sponges" who continually absorb and change. In early childhood classrooms, teachers noticeably deliver their instruction through a combination of verbal and experiential methods, which include adult demonstration, guided practice, and frequent back-and-forth interaction. As demonstrated in the next section, learning environments with younger children are settings that lend themselves to the use of formative assessment with frequent feedback.

Experiential Learning with Targeted Observation

Imagine three early learners working on a project together. The learning target is for students to work cooperatively to sort a basket of assorted shapes into separate piles according to similarities and differences. The activity may include consideration of age-appropriate social behaviors while working on sorting, that is, turn-taking and using materials appropriately during the activity. After giving directions and demonstrating, the teacher allows time for the students to work. As they work, the teacher observes the extent to which they take turns and use the materials appropriately. As the teacher navigates around the room, observing and checking, there are immediate opportunities to record the extent of turn-taking and sharing. This process gives information about how, what, and for whom the teacher may need to apply different interventions. Intervention can be immediate, while the students are working, or through verbal or guided feedback to reteach, redirect, or adapt the task for a particular student or group. *Every Child Shines: Using Formative Assessment to Reflect on Children's Knowledge & Skills* (Institute of Education Services 2019), provides an overview of appropriate practices for gathering information through formative assessment during the early elementary school years.

Strategies for Middle and High School Students

During the secondary school years, curriculum expectations intensify, and concepts become increasingly abstract. The ability to rationalize and problem-solve becomes more critical than during early years or primary education. At this stage, reading in the content areas is vital. The extent of the expectations for writing extensive essays and overall independent functioning significantly increases for secondary students. Frequently their work or projects are not checked until completion, and feedback is untimely. Planning for secondary students' work requires teachers to become even more creative to find formative assessments appropriate for abstract content.

Rubrics

The use of rubrics provides another method that works well for formative assessment (Wolf and Stevens 2007). Rubrics have evolved for use across content areas as tools to provide qualitative information that defines various levels of student performance in a particular area of work. They also explicitly state the task requirements, provide a continuum of expectations from least to most acceptable, and are useful for pointing to information where differentiated instruction is needed (Marzano et al. 2001; Winebrenner & Kiss 2017). Teachers can create rubrics for many content areas. Rubrics help identify and clarify proposed content knowledge and skills and aid teachers and students in gauging the extent of progress toward goal attainment. Using a rubric to identify appropriate feedback and guide discussions is valuable for teacher and peer collaborations.

Figure 3.1 provides an example of a basic rubric to demonstrate the conditions and learning targets that can be applied to gauge how a student is learning a set of skills. In this example, the skills considered relate to following the appropriate steps to solve an equation. Rubrics guide students to reflect on the task expectations, what they have accomplished, and where they need to go next.

In their video *Rubrics for Assessment*, World Learning (2018), presents a process for creating rubrics as tools for formative assessment.

Condition	Not yet meeting target	Progressing to meeting target	Fully meeting target
Effort	Problems not attempted	Attempted to solve several problems	Attempted all problems
Accuracy	Problems solved inaccurately	Followed some steps. Some problems solved accurately	Followed steps. Most to all problems solved accurately
Communication	Work is confusing. Unable to explain or demonstrate steps to solve problems	Able to explain or demonstrate only some steps, but have still solved some problems accurately	Able to explain or demonstrate all the steps, and have solved most to all problems accurately

Fig. 3.1 Sample rubric: learning target—following steps to complete algebra equations

Entrance and Exit Tickets

Another student-directed approach to help teachers quickly gauge students' knowledge at the start and end of a lesson is the use of entrance and exit tickets. This strategy encourages students to take a moment to reflect on their knowledge and expectations and write them down. As the students enter class, they receive a task card, referred to as an "*entrance ticket*," designed to gauge how much they know about the upcoming lesson for the day. The task card may provide a question, an action they must perform, or information they need to think about and share. The students briefly record their answers on their tickets as soon as they are seated. The teacher allows a short period for them to process and write a response. The teacher can review the responses at the start of the class and therefore has information to provide immediate feedback. Similarly, the "*exit ticket*" allows students to perform a task just before the end of the lesson. This gives them time to process and respond to some aspect of the lesson to gain closure and signify its end. Texas based Education Service Center 13 shares several videos to demonstrate these methods. In a video entitled *Teacher Toolkit: Entry Ticket* (2017a), a secondary school teacher discusses using entrance tickets to stimulate thinking about the discussion topic. In a complementary video, *Teacher Toolkit: Exit Ticket Elementary* (2017b), the exit ticket strategy helps primary-aged students exit the lesson by completing a sentence related to the most important thing they learned. The teacher notes that gathering, reading, and addressing the responses help clear up student misconceptions about the teaching and the lesson.

Checklists

Checklists are a valuable tool for explaining skills or task requirements. Checklists provide a road map for teachers to monitor the performance and progress of younger students. Older students can use them to self-monitor their progress toward the learning goal associated with an activity. Checklists can provide the step-by-step guidance and reminders which older students need to complete assignments independently. For younger students, a checklist can take the form of a sequenced list that itemizes the skills expected at various stages of development. A checklist may have more detailed steps appropriate for older students to guide them to complete an activity or project. When conferencing with parents of younger students or directly with older students, the feedback associated with the actions identified on checklists provides insight into strengths and challenges. They also provide substance to help identify and set the teacher's course to modify instruction and gauge student progress. The video, *Assessment in the Classroom: Checklists* (InquireED 2020), provides information regarding the use of checklists to conduct ongoing assessments of young children.

In the video *High School Formative Assessment,* Hatboro-Horsham School District (2014) demonstrates how teachers apply formative assessments to assess and teach older students. The video outlines various strategies, including several which were described earlier in this chapter. The commonality of all the above activities conducted in the video examples is their potential to provide teachers brief but readily available information as they take note of responses and identify for whom, and to what extent, the responses suggest that lesson content and instruction needs to be adapted.

Conclusion

Formative assessments are purposeful events for collecting information to assess learning progress. This chapter proposes that formative assessment must become embedded in the daily and weekly routines of teachers. Planning is essential to the process. Whether working with younger or older students, teachers must prepare assessments and provide feedback that clarifies students' levels of understanding and knowledge about where they are currently and where they are going. In teaching environments often heavily focused on summative assessment, it is important to recognize that well-planned formative assessment is critical to student achievement and should therefore be at the core of the teaching and learning process.

References

Anderson, L. W., Krathwohl, D. R., et al. (Eds.). (2001). *A taxonomy for learning, teaching, and assessing: A revision of Bloom's taxonomy of educational objectives*. Allyn & Bacon.
Australian Institute for Teaching and School Leadership. (2017, August 30). *Formative assessment in the classroom* [Video]. YouTube. https://www.youtube.com/watch?v=9FZR3-l8Y5Y&list =PL1wDoGp0YRMB8W2ENVwK6IWsORTzMncOX.
Barbados Government Information Service. (2019, May 21). Criterion Referenced Test & National Assessment 4 [Video]. YouTube. https://www.youtube.com/watch?v=vrEI-wA48TQ.

Black, P., Harrison, C., Lee, C., Marshall, B., & Wiliam, D. (2004). Working inside the Black box: Assessment for learning in the classroom. *Phi Delta Kappan, 86*(1), 8–21.

Black, P., & Wiliam, D. (2009). Developing the theory of formative assessment. *Educational Assessment, Evaluation and Accountability, 21*(1), 5–31.

Bloom, B. S., & Krathwohl, D. R. (1956). *Taxonomy of educational objectives: The classification of educational goals, by a committee of college and university examiners. Handbook I: Cognitive domain.* Longman.

Chapman, C., & King, R. M. (2012). *Differentiated assessment strategies: One tool does not fit all.* Corwin Press.

Darling-Hammond, L. (2017). Teacher education around the world: What can we learn from international practice? *European Journal of Teacher Education, 40*(3), 291–309.

Education Endowment Foundation. (2021, October 28). *Teaching and Learning Toolkit.* EEF. https://educationendowmentfoundation.org.uk/education-evidence/teaching-learning-toolkit

Education Service Center Region13. (2017a, December 11). *Teacher Toolkit: Entry Ticket* [Video]. YouTube. https://www.youtube.com/watch?v=LEgKEwvIPic

Education Service Center Region13. (2017b, December 11). *Teacher Toolkit: Exit Ticket Elementary* [Video]. YouTube. https://www.youtube.com/watch?v=-pGBBIweGQk

EL Education. (2018, January 17). *Strategies for Monitoring Progress* [Video]. YouTube. https://www.youtube.com/watch?v=0Y9mUVNch2M.

Hatboro-Horsham School District. (2014, May 23). *High School Formative Assessment Video* [Video]. YouTube. https://www.youtube.com/watch?v=BUqK20VRM3w

Hattie, J. (2012). *Visible learning for teachers: Maximizing impact on learning.* Routledge.

Hattie, J., & Timperley, H. (2007). The power of feedback. *Review of Educational Research, 77*(1), 81–112.

Hattie, J., & Zierer, K. (2018). *10 mindframes for visible learning.* NY. Routledge.

Hattie, J. A. C. (2009). *Visible learning: A synthesis of over 800 meta-analyses relating to achievement.* Routledge.

InquireED. (2020, September 22). *Assessment in the Classroom: Checklists* [Video]. YouTube. https://www.youtube.com/watch?v=teevA36QHnc.

Institute of Education Services. (2019, October 29). *Every Child Shines: Using Formative Assessment to Reflect on Children's Knowledge & Skills* [Video]. YouTube. https://www.youtube.com/watch?v=5Q3DFs4hrpU.

Klute, M., Apthorp, H., Harlacher, J., & Reale, M. (2017). *Formative assessment and elementary school student academic achievement: A review of the evidence (REL 2017–259).* U.S. Department of Education, Institute of Education Sciences, National Center for Education Evaluation and Regional Assistance, Regional Educational Laboratory Central. Retrieved from http://ies.ed.gov/ncee/edlabs

Marzano, R. J. (2010). *Designing & teaching learning goals & objectives.* Solution Tree Press.

Marzano, R. J., Pickering, D., & Pollock, J. E. (2001). *Classroom instruction that works: Research-based strategies for increasing student achievement.* ASCD.

Mooney, C. G. (2013). *Theories of childhood: An introduction to Dewey, Montessori, Erikson, Piaget, and Vygotsky* (2nd ed.). Redleaf Press.

Students. *Students.* University of Maryland Press.

Tomlinson, C. (2014). The bridge between Today's lesson and Tomorrow's. *Educational Leadership, 71*, 10–14.

Tomlinson, C. A., & Moon, T. R. (2013). *Assessment and student success in a differentiated classroom.* ASCD.

Wiliam, D. (2017). *Embedded formative assessment* (2nd ed.). Solution Tree Press.

Wiliam, D. (2020a, April 17). *What formative assessment is and isn't* [Video]. YouTube. https://www.youtube.com/watch?v=nfAutEWaqOE

Wiliam, D. (2020b, April 21). *Providing feedback that moves learning forward* [Video]. YouTube. https://www.youtube.com/watch?v=BUPuNc6iYj8

Winebrenner, S., & Kiss, L. (2017). *Teaching kids with learning difficulties in Today's classroom: How every teacher can help struggling students succeed.* Free Spirit.

Wolf, K., & Stevens, E. (2007). The role of rubrics in advancing and assessing student learning. *The Journal of Effective Teaching, 7*(1), 3–14.

World Learning. (2018, January 22). Rubrics for Assessment [Video]. YouTube. https://www.youtube.com/watch?v=kp3rANE8z6s

Chapter 4
Direct Instruction

Abstract This chapter highlights and encourages the use of Direct Instruction (DI) as an evidence-based strategy that helps students participate in instruction with extensive guided practice and opportunities for meaningful review and feedback to refine their understanding as they develop independent skills. This chapter considers that, whether enacted as part of a particular published DI program or embedded more universally in the routine instructional processes and practices of daily instruction, DI approaches are invaluable to student learning. Suggestions are made for ways that DI procedures and practices should work cohesively to improve teaching and learning. In addition, there is a discussion about the strategies aligned with DI principles and the interrelations between effective Direct Instruction and formative assessment.

Rationale

Providing Direct Instruction in reading and math has been found to significantly influence student learning, with students showing improvement in reading comprehension skills and math problem-solving ability (Hattie 2009 2012; Stockard et al. 2018). *Syntheses of meta-analyses* of teaching practices have found that Direct Instruction has an overall average effect size of 0.59, suggesting that education aligned to these practices substantially improves student learning (Hattie 2009). Direct Instruction (DI) supports effective teaching and can be considered an evidence-based practice that includes a specific education plan and a practical teaching model to follow (Hornby 2018). The following resources and commentary serve to provide examples and guidance to help teachers integrate DI strategies into their teaching.

Several critical elements that should be observable in classrooms that apply effective Direct Instruction teaching practices include the following:

- Learning intentions about the specific knowledge and skills to be learned are clear to the teacher and students.

- Teachers build engagement and commitment of students to focus attention on the learning tasks.
- Teachers provide input, model the required functions through examples, and check for students' understanding.
- Individual feedback and remediation occur regularly.
- Key points are reviewed and clarified periodically.
- A clear criterion is established to evaluate the achievement of learning goals.
- Students practice the new learning in different situations to facilitate generalizations.

Historical Development

Direct Instruction evolved from research conducted by Carl Bereiter and Siegfried Engelmann (1966), who studied the impact of direct, guided, repetitive practices on low-achieving students' academic skills. Their techniques incorporated teacher-focused instruction and extensive amounts of purposeful teacher talk that provided a model for students to follow. The model advanced in this initial research found that students developed practical learning skills when they observed the problem-solving stages and when their teachers followed exact steps. Bereiter and Engelmann's approach endorsed the use of guided repetition in mastery learning. Also, it emphasized teacher-directed instruction with time for students to engage in repeated practice until they became independent with specific skills. After 1 year of teaching a group of disadvantaged primary-aged students using this approach, Engelmann found that students involved in the study significantly improved their ability to solve arithmetic problems.

Engelmann's seminal work has continued to be the cornerstone on which more current research and techniques have evolved. Several years after Bereiter and Engelmann's studies in the mid-1960s, the U.S. Department of Education and Office of Economic Opportunity embarked on a large-scale educational experiment called "Project Follow Through." This project sought to identify effective methods to overcome academic gaps observed in impoverished children. The first 10 years of this project from 1967 to 1977 involved 200,000 students and compared the effects of various programs, including Direct Instruction, on the students' academic, affective, and cognitive skills. Compared to students who received non-Direct Instruction programs, the students who received Direct Instruction demonstrated the most favorable academic achievement, problem-solving skills, and self-confidence (Meyer et al. 1983). Later studies continued to show the positive effects of these programs across diverse demographics, particularly with disadvantaged and special education populations (Adams & Engelmann 1996; Kinder et al. 2005).

Overview of Direct Instruction Programs

Published Programs

Several Direct Instruction programs evolved from the research of Engelmann. Today many of these programs are marketed through the National Institute for Direct Instruction (NIFDI), which identifies its programs as unique due to their focus on a specific curriculum, instructional programs, and materials associated with Engelmann's methods. The Direct Instructional System for *Teaching and Remediation (DISTAR) Arithmetic* and *DISTAR Reading*, *Corrective Math*, *Reading Mastery, Funnix Reading*, and *Funnix Math* are several examples of specific published programs. Published programs, along with lesson samples, can be reviewed on *NIFDI's website*. This website refers to their Direct Instruction programs by identifying them with a capitalized "Direct Instruction" (DI). In this manner, they distinguish themselves from other similar teaching approaches that incorporate other researchers' findings and recommendations. Published DI programs include materials that teachers utilize for pre- and post-assessments, presentation books, charts to support pre-teaching, guided lessons, pacing charts, and activities to give students practice. These materials ensure uniformity of practice by providing resources to establish consistency.

An example from The Association for Direct Instruction (ADI) (2013a) demonstrates the use of a DI program to teach reading skills. The video is entitled *Reading Mastery Training Series: Video 4—Countdown to Lesson One.* In this example, the teacher starts with instruction on letter sounds, advancing to words, and eventually to entire stories. Visual charts and a detailed teaching script provide for consistent delivery according to the expectations of the program. The teacher starts the lesson by first providing examples to introduce individual letter sounds and blends. This is done by presenting a model or demonstration of the sound and then guiding students to repeat in unison as they orally practice the sound or word. The students take turns reproducing the sounds while simultaneously following an associated video. The teachers' visual charts, scripted presentation guides, and verbal and nonverbal signals are examples of scaffolded instruction which is discussed later in this chapter. The students can practice as a group and individually, while teachers offer verbal encouragement to maintain their engagement. Scaffolds are removed as mastery of skills occurs. The teachers reference the importance of conducting instruction in small groups to maximize student involvement and turn-taking. Students move beyond the basics from relating letters to sounds to reading words and then passages. They are encouraged to read independently to the teacher or their peers.

Principles of Direct Instruction

Many tenets of Direct Instruction (DI) are incorporated within the classification of what are regarded to be effective teaching and cognitive strategies. Over time, additional considerations relevant to teachers' knowledge and recommended practices have evolved. These practices have focused on the importance of clarifying expectations at all stages of the instruction process, the need for providing regular feedback to students, and the provision of scaffolded instruction (Marzano 2007; Rosenshine 2012; Rosenshine & Stevens 1986). Scaffolded learning provides support based on students' needs and then slowly releases the support as students demonstrate that they acquire content and are independent with skills. Specific examples of scaffolded instruction are discussed later in this chapter. Teaching programs developed around guided learning and mastery teaching models also share many of the practices associated with Direct Instruction.

Research on teacher effectiveness has advanced several significant concepts from DI. Effective instruction must focus on the interactions between the teacher, the student, and the content. Teachers must find ways to keep students engaged in the learning process while exploring curriculum content and building skills. As students become independent with academic and social skills, they must also develop self-monitoring skills. Therefore, teachers must facilitate a learning process in which assessment gauges both teacher and student success.

Identifying where students are currently functioning and providing them content materials appropriate to their levels is foundational to effective teaching. Teachers need to consider this as they provide models to show students how to complete tasks and present them with appropriate guided experiences. Activities, projects, worksheets, and reading materials at suitable levels are provided to students to give them extensive practice.

The video, *Reading Mastery Training Series: Video 1_Path to Literacy* (ADI 2013b), depicts the extent of the teacher's direct guidance. It summarizes the importance of in-depth teacher knowledge about the content and methods appropriate for teaching essential reading skills. Five teachers share their experiences teaching primary students to read and summarize their steps, using a DI program, *Reading Mastery*, to develop reading skills.

Strategies that align with DI can occur within all stages of a lesson. Teachers must anticipate and plan ways to directly intervene with students before, during, and after the lesson. For example, interventions may include taking time to engage students in probing conversation on a topic or problem, completing a brief word association game, brainstorming, jotting down thoughts, or observing a video or audio example.

Classroom Practices

Direct Instruction approaches to teaching involve stages, emphasizing how teachers present and monitor the lessons, and how they participate in the task. The practices alluded to so far are necessary to successful lessons. Successful teachers use methods developed based on research, and in so doing, they are more equipped to engage in effective practices that help students learn difficult tasks (Hattie 2009, 2012; Rosenshine 2012). Rosenshine's (2012) evidence-based practices include:

- Beginning each lesson with a review
- Asking many questions to check for understanding
- Presenting new material in small steps with practice after each step
- Giving clear and detailed instructions and explanations
- Demonstrating actions such as "think aloud" and modeling steps for students to follow
- Creating examples and reference materials of completed work and problem solutions
- Limiting the number of materials students receive at one time
- Providing a high level of active practice for all students
- Asking students to explain what they have learned
- Checking the responses of all students
- Providing systematic feedback and corrections
- Allowing time for re-explanation of information
- Preparing students for independent practice
- Monitoring students when they begin independent practice
- Reteaching material when necessary
- Using frequent and varied formative assessments

Teachers need to monitor their practices as they plan and implement the various lesson stages. A checklist or goal setting chart is a useful way for teachers to self-monitor their practices. Figure 4.1 provides examples of teacher and student roles within a Direct Instruction collaboration, outlining several of the effective practices discussed throughout this chapter.

Planning for Instruction

Teachers need a clear plan to organize and deliver lessons. At this stage plans must include strategies for engaging students and determining existing levels of understanding. They must identify the content to be addressed and clarify what students must know and do. Planning should also include methods for assessing incremental progress and giving feedback. Assessment information helps teachers tailor instructional content and delivery to the appropriate skill levels of their students (Pinchock & Brandt 2009).

Direct instruction processes and practices	Teacher should...	Student should...
Review	• Ask questions to stimulate thinking. • Provide review activities to help students to activate prior knowledge. • Review and clarify the objectives/learning intentions.	• Share what they already know about the content. • Ask questions if they do not understand the content or expectations.
Presentation	• Divide activity/tasks into several incremental steps. • Create activities appropriate for students to practice during and after the lesson. • Explain sequentially and in detail how to complete tasks/activities. • Show/demonstrate to students how to complete tasks/activities. • Talk aloud to demonstrate the thinking process as tasks/activities are completed. • Guide students as they practice the tasks/activities along with the teacher. • Provide a completed sample as a reference for students to follow. • Prepare activities and allow time for students to practice on their own. • Plan alternative strategies and scaffolded instruction activities that may be necessary for re-teaching.	• Observe demonstrations and listen to explanations about content, tasks, and activities. • Participate in and complete activities related to tasks/activities. • Use and follow demonstrations and visual samples to help complete tasks and activities-first along with the teacher and then independently. • Practice thinking out loud while completing tasks and activities. • Ask questions when the information is confusing or unclear. • Communicate with teachers and peers about work assignments.

Fig. 4.1 Examples of teacher and student roles within a Direct Instruction collaboration

Planning and assessing	• Plan a list of appropriate questions to ask at different stages of the lesson. • Identify verbal and nonverbal ways for students to demonstrate understanding and prepare appropriate assessments (e.g., orally explain/discuss/draw/write /complete a chart/identify true-false statements/complete a quiz) • Listen to and observe student responses for accuracy. • Give students corrective feedback (during and after task completion) to determine progress and needs. • Check-in periodically with students who seem to be challenged by the tasks/activities. • Build time into the lesson for further explanation and re-teaching as needed.	• Think about answers to questions and respond individually. • Discuss questions and responses with a peer. • Jot bulleted points or write a statement to respond to questions. • Draw a picture/chart to depict a response. • Share responses to questions, tasks, and activities with teachers/peers. • Complete a quiz. • Listen to feedback from teachers/peers. • Use feedback to confirm progress or to apply a different approach to improve accuracy with the tasks/activities.

Fig. 4.1 (continued)

Students' Existing Knowledge and Skills

It is necessary to understand what students already know and what their skill levels are at the outset. Knowledge about what students know and can do provides invaluable information to help teachers. Popham (2003) suggests that teachers must think through and plan ways to gather prior knowledge to operationalize their planning and next steps. For example, to get an idea of the extent to which students can determine the main idea, they may be required to read a paragraph and respond in various ways. Either write a statement to explain the paragraph's main argument or select an appropriate response from several options provided, or verbalize their response to a peer partner. The next logical step is to review the responses and identify precisely how students appear to be processing what they read. From that information, teachers can more accurately identify the next steps.

In the absence of programs that provide pre- and post-assessments, teachers frequently create their own assessments. It is important to note that pre- and post-assessment does not always involve a paper test, and neither do assessments have to be lengthy. For example, teachers can gather student data by asking questions, gathering oral responses, or listening and making notes as students share ideas with a partner. Teachers can ask students to complete two or three math problems or word matches to check their understanding. These actions to gauge understanding may occur at the start or end of the lesson and are valuable to allow periodic checks for understanding. The key is to get information about what students know, what planning and problem-solving processes they are applying, and what content and skills they find challenging.

Engaging Students

To fully engage students, the starting point of lessons should incorporate actions on the teacher's part to clarify the learning targets or goals and use strategies that support review and linking of prior learning (Marzano 2004; Rosenshine 2012). At this stage, communication about the lesson topic and what students must know should be explicit. Teachers should also use various data collection methods to identify students' knowledge by asking them to jot down words or thoughts, draw a picture, or verbally share responses with a partner. Asking students to identify things they want to learn, and questions they may have, also helps them process and organize their thoughts and ideas.

The video, *Sing Those Strategies!: Engaging Students in Reading Comprehension Strategies* (Balanced Literacy Diet 2012), demonstrates a strategy for engagement and lesson introduction conducted at the elementary level. Focusing on reading comprehension, the teacher identifies five different comprehension strategies (visualization/inferencing/summarizing/predicting/prior knowledge), which students can use. The teacher presents a visual chart of the strategies, explains each, and provides examples to clarify what each approach means. The teacher asks questions to probe the students' understanding of the terminology on the chart and engages them in verbal sharing to determine their current knowledge. The teacher also maintains student engagement by having them participate actively in a song about the strategies. In their video entitled *Introducing a New Unit*, National Geographic Learning (2015) demonstrates how a teacher involves primary students in visually analyzing pictures in a text to activate students' prior knowledge and make predictions. Students analyze a picture and share their perceptions about what they see. Along with the picture, the teacher provides verbal clues to help encourage student responses and further engages them through questioning to determine what they already know.

Adapting to the Needs of Older Students

The above engagement and lesson introduction methods are appropriate at the primary and secondary levels, although the content's complexity may vary. For example, at the secondary level, within a literature or history textbook, where there are fewer picture representations, the teacher may have the students skim a page to look for character names, dates, or events. Based on that information, students can reflect on and share thoughts or make predictions about what the dates and events suggest about the content, and genre of the text. Though students may be older, these engagement strategies and the linking of prior knowledge are still necessary and are adaptable to the curriculum content.

During the Lesson

Setting Learning Intentions

This next stage focuses on structured actions that set the context for new learning by introducing new concepts to be learned. Expectations about what students are to do and how to do it are explicitly stated and demonstrated to avoid uncertainty about the associated tasks. Information gathered during formative assessment (see Chap. 3) is critical to determining and setting these intentions.

For example, when teaching a unit on argumentative writing, the teacher provides a written guide or example to outline the intention of the task. The specified objective may be to write a five-sentence paragraph in which the first sentence states the position taken, the second through fourth sentence provides details to support the argument, and the final sentence rationalizes how the details provided support the position taken. After the students select a topic and complete their initial drafts, they are encouraged to share their paragraph. Notably, the learning intentions are specific, the students know what to do, and the teacher then moves around and guides them individually as they work on the task. Additional assessment strategies that can be incorporated into the Direct Instruction lesson include:

- Periodic checks for understanding: Orally question students about information learned so far and things about which they are still wondering.
- Requesting students to develop, record, and post questions and new learning statements on a "parking lot": The teacher intermittently selects an item from the parking lot to share, review, or clarify as appropriate.
- Allowing 1 min to do a "quick write" to scribe some of the main points they have learned: 3–5 min can then be allowed for sharing and clarification in large or small groups as the teacher monitors students to determine the extent of their understanding.

Scaffolded Instruction

Students require actual experiences and exposure to learning aids or tools which can be used and later removed. Vygotsky's (1978) research on student learning encouraged practices focused on building support structures to help students process and learn information. This teaching practice is referred to as "scaffolded instruction" and originated from studies on the effect of adult support in helping children to develop independent skills (Wood, Bruner & Ross 1976). Scaffolded instruction occurs when teachers provide supports or scaffolds, such as materials or various teaching aids, which students can use to help develop, refine, and extend their knowledge and skills. Scaffolds can range from verbal or visual supports to materials and instructional props and activities. Direct Instruction incorporates scaffolds that allow students to observe others completing tasks, listen to the steps and tips they give, and follow along while individually attempting to complete the task and reach the target goal. Scaffolded supports are temporary and are removed as the individual learns to accomplish the task independently. An appropriate analogy to explain scaffolding is the use of training wheels to support a child as they practice the skill of riding a bicycle. As they master balance, the wheels are removed. If balancing issues return later, the training wheels can be reconnected as needed. Similarly, if students show regression in the classroom or have difficulty with new learning, it is sometimes necessary to reintroduce scaffolding strategies to help them overcome their learning challenges.

Outlined below are several strategies to support scaffolded instruction:

- Provide verbal prompts to aid students with learning facts or routines.
- Utilize concept mapping (see Chap. 7) to help organize ideas when planning a story or research project.
- Create and explain visual reference charts to depict sequences toward solving a math problem or science project.
- Develop "to-do" lists or checklists to remind students about the rules and steps of a learning process.
- Establish visual schedules to remind students of their daily activities.
- Provide vocabulary lists or word lists to help students practice and recall information and facts.

Scaffolding strategies are apparent in the increasing use of various social media applications, such as YouTube videos which teach individuals to complete projects and tasks independently. Their value is relevant to the classroom, where learners require and respond to different instructional formats that make tasks more manageable.

Demonstration and Modeling

Direct Instruction incorporates teaching by demonstration. This involves guiding students through a process of "I do, we do, you do." The "I do" stage consists of the teacher modeling the activity. In the "we do" phase, the teacher supports students in performing the exercise with guidance. In the "you do" stage, students independently perform the activity. It is essential to recognize that it often takes multiple iterations of the "I do, we do, you do" process for some students to develop independence and mastery. If assessments demonstrate the need, it may be necessary to return to the prior stage before continuing. This assures support for those students who need either reteaching or exposure to alternative strategies to help them establish a foundation. For these reasons, observations and information gathered during the guided practice, feedback, and verification of instruction are essential. These stages of the process encourage teachers to reflect on and adjust their approaches based on student performance.

During the "I do" stage of the lesson, students must observe as the teacher demonstrates and explains the task they are to perform. Teacher demonstration at the start of a learning task provides additional perspectives that can help clarify students' expectations and understanding. This is just as critical for older students as it is during the early years of instruction.

Demonstration and modeling can take various forms, such as teachers role-playing the actions and words needed to fulfill a task or showing how to use a reference chart, problem-solving matrix, or instructional video. Following the demonstrations, students should be encouraged to apply the processes they observe to solve problems as a group and eventually use them independently. This phase's critical step is to provide information about procedures and content that students can think about and refer to as they start to make connections with prior knowledge.

In the video entitled *Eighth Grade Literature Study Lesson* (Williams 2013), a secondary-level teacher practices engagement and modeling to teach students vocabulary words associated with emotions. She first explains and demonstrates through "thinking aloud" as she identifies an emotion associated with her selected color. The teacher also explained why the selected color makes her feel a particular emotion. Students observed this process and were then asked to take turns doing the same. Throughout the video, the teacher guides students through the lesson sequence by asking questions, stopping to give examples, and then asking questions that encourage them to reflect and share. The teacher later connects the students' discussion about emotions to the emotional experiences in a book they are currently reading.

Guided Practice

During guided practice, the teacher works alongside students as they practice the focus activity. In Direct Instruction, this is referred to as the "we do" stage. This practice time is nonjudgmental and represents a time when students can make mistakes. Mistakes are viewed as valuable steps along the path to becoming better. Frequently teachers build opportunities for students to practice as a group and, in so doing, provide opportunities for cooperative learning exchanges so that students can also learn from each other. Guided practice as a strategy evolved from research, suggesting that students should be taught within a development zone in which the instruction and content are neither too easy nor beyond the students' abilities. Vygotsky (1978) refers to this as the Zone of Proximal Development to explain that the appropriate level of instruction is the developmental zone in which the student can do the task when a little help is provided. At this stage, there are opportunities for guided practice as the teacher observes and assists students. This is also an appropriate time to give feedback to students.

The video, *Science guided.mp4* (Fisher and Frey 2012), demonstrates how a high school science teacher practices guided instruction as part of a physics lesson. The teacher interacts with small groups to provide verbal prompts and give feedback to assist with understanding the lesson. After exposure to the relevant strategies and skills modeled through demonstration, students are able to better understand how to effectively plan and execute the actions needed to work through a designated task. The guided practice activities allow students to participate and have multiple opportunities to practice before venturing on to tackle the task individually. During guided practice, the teacher navigates the class to monitor and provide support with verbal reminders and prompting as needed. Along with frequent practice opportunities, students need time for asking questions, discussing, and sharing as they work together to problem-solve. At this stage, teachers provide frequent feedback and additional guidance to clarify and reteach as needed. Teachers need to be keen observers and assessors of students' performance to gauge which students are successful and which require additional support or different teaching approaches.

Independent Practice

With independence and mastery as the goal, this stage allows students to work on assignments or projects independently. During the "you do" phase of explicit instruction, the intention is to encourage independence while providing a high degree of practice. For example, scaffolding during instruction may have included a checklist or reference list outlining the steps and expectations for a task. Students need encouragement to use these tools to self-check their accuracy and progress on tasks as they build confidence to work independently and become efficient with self-regulation.

Feedback and Verification

During all phases of Direct Instruction, there are opportunities for teachers to engage in feedback. Effective Direct Instruction requires teachers to be keen observers as they both teach and assess the extent to which students are performing. The effective use of feedback is a critical component of effective teaching. Students need feedback about the tasks they have completed, the process they underwent to complete the task, and feedback to guide what they will do to enhance progress (see Chap. 3). Additionally, useful and practical feedback is appropriately determined and provided in conjunction with formative assessments, which give valuable insights about students and their work within the context of instruction (Black & Wiliam 1998). Teachers should provide feedback at the task level, communicating with students about what they are doing correctly, what they are doing incorrectly, and specific guidance about steps they need to follow to redo their task according to their recommendation. Feedback should be given close to task completion to enable students to process their actions and make needed changes with immediacy. Feedback should let students know where they are performing relative to the goals for the assignment. They must also be encouraged to become active participants in the feedback process and to self-reflect and self-evaluate to monitor their progress and their needs. Teachers should use this information to reflect on their instructional practices, the extent to which their techniques were effective, and the need to adjust practices if current strategies are not working. Wiliam (2016) (see Chap. 3) suggests the following strategies to assist teachers with providing useful feedback:

- Recognize that feedback is of value when students use it to improve performance.
- Keep the purpose of the feedback in mind.
- Give feedback that students can use.
- Assign tasks that illuminate students' thinking.
- Provide feedback that encourages students to go back and look at their work more closely and analytically. For example, allow them to locate the errors themselves and fix them.
- Teach students how to self-assess.
- Develop relationships that foster trust and increase the likelihood of positive perceptions about the feedback.

The examples that follow describe several strategies that align with Direct Instruction models for teaching. These examples represent how the teacher can apply practical steps, even in the absence of a published program. The examples emphasize teacher direction with a gradual reduction of responsibility as students move from guided practice to independence.

Direct Instruction Strategies for Preschool and Elementary Students

When young learners are actively engaged in formal instruction routines during the preschool years, they benefit and learn through interactive opportunities that provide exposure to various literacy experiences (Clay 2001; Fountas & Pinnell 1996). In the more formative years of preschool and kindergarten, students observe and participate in motor tasks, cognitive and social tasks, and activities that encourage them to communicate verbally. At this stage, there tends to be frequent "teacher talk" with frequent repetition of expectations. Steps and directions for task completion tend to be specific and sequential. Primary-aged students tend to ask teachers many questions as they seek clarity and validation for their actions. Much of how students learn in these early years aligns well with Direct Instruction precepts, focusing on learning through modeled, guided experiences with a high level of practice opportunities. This is exemplified by the teaching strategies embodied in Reading Recovery.

Reading Recovery

Reading Recovery, mentioned in Chap. 1, is an evidence-based practice that embodies Direct Instruction methodology. Hattie's (2009) book reported Reading Recovery to have an above-average impact on children's achievement levels, with an effect size of 0.5. The Best Evidence Encyclopedia includes Reading Recovery in the list of "Top-Rated" reading programs with "strong evidence of effectiveness." The What Works Clearinghouse reports that Reading Recovery has the highest overall effectiveness rating for general reading achievement of all the 26 beginning reading programs reviewed. Therefore, Reading Recovery is a program with a very strong base in research evidence.

Reading Recovery was developed during the 1970s and has been researched and implemented in many countries around the world, including New Zealand, England, and the USA, where it has been in operation for over 30 years (Clay 1995; Holliman & Hurry 2013). It is a short-term program that provides tutoring to the lowest achieving children struggling with reading and writing after their first year at school. Trained Reading Recovery teachers deliver teaching one-to-one in daily 30-min pullout sessions over 12–20 weeks. The program is supplementary to mainstream classroom literacy instruction and aims to foster the development of reading and writing strategies by tailoring individualized lessons to each student's needs.

Clay (1995) laid out specific teaching strategies to be used at each of the program's four phases: first, *Learning About Direction*: locating responses, spatial layout, and learning to look at print; second, *Writing Stories*: hearing and recording sounds in words and assembling cutup stories; third, *Reading Books*: choice of book, orientation to the story before reading, teaching during the first reading, teaching after the first reading, reading for fluency, home and school practice, and second reading of the book next day; and fourth, *Teaching for Strategies*: linking sound sequence with letter sequence, taking words apart in reading, and teaching for phrasing in fluent reading. Some of these strategies are illustrated in the video, which is entitled *Key Stage 1/2 English, Episode 2: Reading Recovery: One-to-One* (Newbubbles Ltd. (2012a).

Another video explains how implementing a Reading Recovery Program in a school can support a whole-school approach to literacy development through the Reading Recovery teacher involving other teachers in the school and the parents of children in the program. In this way the teaching approach and strategies included in Reading Recovery can benefit the whole school. This assumes that, as is the case with any evidence-based practice introduced into schools, it is compatible with the education system in which it is used, and the practical realities of the school, including available professional expertise and supportive stakeholder perspectives. The video is entitled *Key Stage 1/2 English, Episode 1: Reading Recovery: A Whole School Approach* (Newbubbles Ltd. 2012b).

Shared Reading

Shared reading is an approach to developing early literacy by engaging young readers in the reading process by listening and responding to guided participation as a story is read to them (Holdaway 1979). The reader engages the listener by actively reading with expression and intonation during shared reading. The reader intermittently pauses to ask questions and highlight various parts of the text. During shared reading, the reader conducts a read-aloud to listeners. This provides a model for the students to follow. Beginning readers are encouraged to mimic or repeat the sounds, words, and eventually phrases and sentences. When the reader asks questions and models the correct response, they are engaging in guided instruction. As the students interact with the adult reader, they should be given opportunities to pretend to read independently. Even efforts to say things in their own words while looking at the pages represent efforts toward independence. This strategy aligns with the Direct Instruction approach symbolized by demonstration, engagement, and opportunities to practice with guidance through interaction with the teacher. Shared reading is demonstrated in the video example, entitled *Chicka, Chicka, Boom, Boom: Shared Reading in Kindergarten* (Balanced Literacy Diet 2011) which shows a teacher conducting a shared reading lesson with primary students.

Strategies for Middle and High School Students

Scaffolding with Socratic Circles

Scaffolded instruction, as discussed earlier in the chapter, is integral to effective guided instruction and Direct Instruction. A video example from Edutopia (2018), entitled *Scaffolding Discussion Skills With a Socratic Circle*, features Linda Darling-Hammond, explaining how a secondary school teacher engages students in a Socratic discussion on a challenging topic. The goal is for students to become involved and take turns participating in the conversation by using the reading materials provided to gather information and evidence to help them formulate responses to a discussion question. The teacher scaffolds the reading by providing reading passages on the same topic, but at varying reading levels to accommodate different ability levels. Students are given time to prepare for the discussion by reading independently, reflecting on a question, and jotting down evidence from their readings to help them with input for the discussion. Some students take turns sharing, others are encouraged to make notes from the input from others, and some are encouraged to track the discussion and share what they have understood from their peers. The scaffolds increase the likelihood that more students will be involved if they are allowed different ways to participate.

Explicit Instruction

Explicit instruction is direct and intentional teaching. Explicit instruction involves teachers using the three-phase approach described earlier in this chapter. In the first phase, referred to as the "I do" phase, the teacher models and demonstrates while the students observe. During the second "we do" phase of this process, students practice together with direct, guided support and feedback from the teacher. Third, students are encouraged to complete the task independently during the "you do" phase. With explicit instruction, no aspect of the lesson is left to chance. The expectations, task steps, and strategies for problem-solving related to the content, concepts, and skills are explicitly shown and clearly stated to the students (Archer & Hughes 2011; McLeskey et al. 2017).

The video, *I Do, We Do, You Do: Scaffolding Reading Comprehension in Social Studies* (American Graduate 2012), demonstrates explicit teaching of reading comprehension. In the example, portions of a text are read aloud by the teacher as she demonstrates her comprehension process by thinking aloud. She verbalizes what she observes and then makes notes on a graphic organizer as she looks at the pictures. The teacher then encourages the students to practice making notes on their graphic organizers as they work with a partner. This is an example of the teacher providing scaffolded instruction as students practice the skills needed to organize their thoughts and information.

Conclusion

Direct Instruction is explicit and, as such, relies on teacher-guided lessons, with a high emphasis on teacher direction, which gradually fades to independence. Direct Instruction relies on accurate information about current knowledge and skills to project accurate determinations about moving students to the next level of complexity. Assessment is frequent, and typically students do not move on to the next step until they have developed some degree of mastery at the current one. Teacher interventions during Direct Instruction are targeted and allow students to observe task completion steps in action, practice the steps with guidance, and then practice independently to work toward mastery.

Whether using materials and products from a published program or applying the Direct Instruction model to generic teaching platforms, the associated strategies can be effectively implemented as part of evidence-based practices demonstrated to improve the effectiveness of instruction. Under this model, scaffolded instruction, guided teaching, feedback for verification, and practice opportunities all contribute to the planning and delivery of meaningful lessons.

References

Adams, G., & Engelmann, S. (1996). *Research on direct instruction: 25 years beyond DISTAR*. Educational Achievement Systems.

American Graduate DC. (2012, April 30). *I do, we do, you do: Scaffolding reading comprehension in social studies [Video]*. YouTube. https://www.youtube.com/watch?v=gleNo8dqHb8

Archer, A. L., & Hughes, C. (2011). *Explicit instruction: Effective and efficient teaching*. Guilford Press.

Association for Direct Instruction. (2013a, September 19). *Reading mastery training series: Video 4_countdown to lesson one [Video]*. YouTube. https://www.youtube.com/watch?v=O-obRARe6MI&t=10s

Association for Direct Instruction. (2013b, September 19). *Reading mastery training series: Video 1_path to literacy [Video]*. YouTube. https://www.youtube.com/watch?v=2cgoqI8OWEs

Bereiter, C., & Engelmann, S. (1966). *Teaching disadvantaged children in the preschool*. Prentice-Hall.

Black, P., & Wiliam, D. (1998). Inside the Black box: Raising standards through classroom assessment. *Phi Delta Kappan, 80*, 139–148.

Clay, M. M. (1995). *Reading recovery: A guidebook for teachers in training*. Heinemann.

Clay, M. M. (2001). *Change over time in children's literacy development*. Heinemann.

Edutopia. (2018, November 16). *Scaffolding discussion skills with a socratic circle [Video]*. YouTube. https://www.youtube.com/watch?v=e3IBLKYaK1E

Fisher and Frey. (2012, March 20). *Science guided.mp4 [Video]*. YouTube. https://www.youtube.com/watch?v=JxR1jMjn-nE

Fountas, I. C., & Pinnell, G. S. (1996). *Guided Reading, good first teaching for all children*. Heinemann.

Hattie, J. (2012). *Visible learning for teachers: Maximizing impact on learning*. Routledge.

Hattie, J. A. C. (2009). *Visible learning: A synthesis of over 800 meta-analyses relating to achievement*. Routledge.

Holdaway, D. (1979). *The foundations of literacy*. Ashton Scholastic.

Holliman, A. J., & Hurry, J. (2013). The effects of Reading recovery on children's literacy progress and special educational needs status: A three-year follow-up study. *Educational Psychology, 33*(6), 719–733.

Hornby, G. (2018). Eight key evidence-based teaching strategies for all levels of education. *Australian Education Leader, 40*(4), 28–31.

Kinder, D., Kubina, R., & Marchand-Martella, N. (2005). Special education and direct instruction: An effective combination. *Journal of Direct Instruction, 5*(1), 1–36.

Marzano, R. (2004). *Building background knowledge for academic achievement: Research on what works in schools*. ASCAD.

Marzano, R. J. (2007). *The art and science of teaching: A comprehensive framework for effective instruction*. ASCD.

McLeskey, J., Barringer, M. D., Billingsley, B., Brownell, M., Jackson, D., Kennedy, M., Lewis, T., Maheady, L., Rodriguez, J., Scheeler, M. C., Winn, J., & Ziegler, D. (2017). *High-leverage practices in special education.* Council for Exceptional Children & CEEDAR Center.

Meyer, L., Gersten, R., & Gutkin, J. (1983). Direct instruction: A project follow through success story in an Inner-City school. *The Elementary School Journal, 84*(2), 241–252.

National Geographic Learning. (2015, September 14). *Introducing a new unit [Video].* YouTube. https://www.youtube.com/watch?v=nAQGIrMyb38

Newbubbles Ltd. (2012a, June 4). *Series: KS1/2 English, episode 2: Reading recovery: One-to-one, 2008, 13:51 mins [Video].* YouTube. https://www.youtube.com/watch?v=M0RSHM_x664

Newbubbles Ltd. (2012b, June 4). *Series: KS1/2 English, episode 1: Reading recovery: A whole school approach, 2008, 13:51 mins [Video].* YouTube. https://www.youtube.com/watch?v=nz-BYmjZHrw

Pinchok, N., & Brandt, W. C. (2009). *Connecting formative assessment research to practice: An introductory guide for educators.* Learning Point Associates.

Popham, W. J. (2003). *Test better, teach better: The instructional role of assessment.* Association for Supervision and Curriculum Development.

Rosenshine, B. (2012). Principles of instruction: Research-based strategies that all teachers should know. *American Educator, 39,* 12–19.

Rosenshine, B., & Stevens, R. (1986). Teaching functions. *Handbook of Research on Teaching, 3,* 376–391.

Stockard, J., Wood, T. W., Coughlin, C., & Rasplica Khoury, C. (2018). The effectiveness of direct instruction curricula: A meta-analysis of a half-century of research. *Review of Educational Research, 88*(4), 479–507.

The Balanced Literacy Diet. (2011, December 30). *Chicka, chicka, boom, boom: Shared reading in kindergarten [Video].* YouTube. https://www.youtube.com/watch?v=MtHGI6irkpI&t=13s

The Balanced Literacy Diet. (2012, February 13). *Sing those strategies!: Engaging students in reading comprehension strategies [Video].* YouTube. https://www.youtube.com/watch?v=wxIZmgrK-xc

Vygotsky, L. S. (1978). *Mind in society: The development of higher psychological processes.* Harvard University Press.

Wiliam, D. (2016). The secret of effective feedback. *Educational Leadership, 73,* 10–15.

Williams, J. L. (2013, June 18). *Eighth grade literature study lesson [Video].* YouTube. https://www.youtube.com/watch?v=P4rWZrgyCbs

Wood, D. J., Bruner, J. S., & Ross, G. (1976). The role of tutoring in problem solving. *The Journal of Child Psychology and Psychiatry, 17,* 89–100.

Chapter 5
Cooperative Learning

Abstract Cooperative learning is discussed based on findings that the instructional use of small groups, in which students work together to maximize their own and each other's learning, optimizes both social and academic outcomes. However, it is made clear that simply working in small groups does not constitute cooperative learning. What makes cooperative learning different from other types of group work are two fundamental elements, positive interdependence and individual accountability. These elements are described for their importance as critical components of effective cooperative interactions. Strategies to aid teachers with developing and maintaining cooperative classrooms are discussed and cooperative instructional activities to engage student participation and facilitate learning are outlined.

Rationale

The term "cooperative learning" is typically used to define the instructional use of small groups in which students work together to maximize their own and each other's learning (Johnson and Johnson 1991). Cooperative learning has been found to be one of the most effective class-wide interventions in education, with an average effect size of 0.59 compared with individual learning being reported by Hattie (2009). Furthermore, cooperative strategies such as the jigsaw method, described later in the chapter, are reported to have an effect size of 1.2 on Hattie's *Visible Learning website*.

Three of the primary developers of cooperative learning, Johnson and Johnson (1991), Kagan (1994), and Slavin (1995), all define cooperative learning in terms that exclude simply working in small groups, to make it clear that not all group work constitutes cooperative learning. What makes cooperative learning different from other types of group work are the two fundamental elements: positive interdependence and individual accountability. The developers above insist that cooperative learning can only flourish when there is individual accountability and positive interdependence linked to group rewards or goals. The video, made by Robert Slavin, entitled *Basics of Cooperative Learning* (Learning for Justice 2012), notes the importance of these key elements and outlines some of the benefits of cooperative learning.

Individual accountability is present when each student's performance is assessed, and the results are provided to the individual and the group (Johnson, Johnson, & Holubec 2013). Additionally, individual accountability requires that every team member be accountable for completing tasks so that no one can "hitchhike" on the work of others (Ning & Hornby 2010). When students are clear about their accountability, they are more likely to engage in active participation and feel motivated to learn. Therefore, students in cooperative learning groups are likely to engage in more effort and take greater responsibility for their learning outcomes since they are clear that their contribution to teamwork can be individually identified and assessed (Hornby 2009).

Positive interdependence is present when students perceive that they can reach their learning goals, if and only if the other students in their group also reach their goals. It involves linking students together so individuals cannot succeed unless all group members succeed (Johnson et al. 2013). Incorporating positive interdependence into group work facilitates mutual support and cooperation among team members (Brown & Thomson 2000). Positive interdependence also generates peer norms favoring achievement, increasing peer interaction, quantity and quality of learning, and creating a supportive and less stressful learning environment.

An examination of numerous research studies indicates that cooperative learning strategies lead to higher academic achievement than an individual or a competitive approach (Johnson et al. 2013; Kyndt et al. 2013). This is the case for high- and low-ability students, students of all ages, and a wide range of subject areas in the curriculum. It has also been found that cooperative learning has positive social and motivational effects (Sachar & Sharan 1995).

The term cooperative learning describes a wide range of different intervention strategies, including "jigsaw" (Aronson & Patnoe 1997), "student teams achievement divisions" (Slavin 1995), "numbered heads together" (Kagan 1994), and "group investigation" (Sharan & Sharan 1990). With examples presented at the end of this chapter, these well-known strategies have extensive research evidence supporting their effectiveness. They are used in various classrooms with a wide range of age groups which illustrates that cooperative learning provides a treasure trove of strategies that facilitate optimum learning outcomes and is considered a key evidence-based teaching strategy. This is illustrated in a video from Kagan (2009), entitled *Kagan Cooperative Learning-Structures for Success Part 1*.

Theory

Research on group interactions conducted by Kurt Lewin (1947) demonstrated that individuals alter their behavior when participating in group activities. Lewin's study identified groups as dynamic entities in which individuals within a group tend to develop interdependence. Earlier research, based on Lev Vygotsky's zones of proximal development, posited that individuals at a particular developmental stage of learning gain significant knowledge and skills when they have an opportunity to interact with others who have already obtained these skills and knowledge (Doolittle 1995). These are some of the foundational tenets which advanced cooperative interactions as a practical approach to learning.

Cooperative teaching and learning represent a break from the traditional whole-class instruction and a move toward structured small group encounters designed to produce quality work under conditions that encourage students and are seen as valuable to the individual members and the group. As a teaching method, cooperative learning positively impacts students' academic achievement and social development (Gillies 2016; Hattie 2012; Johnson & Johnson 1991). Effective implementation of cooperative learning strategies requires the presentation and nurturing of five key elements: positive interdependence, individual accountability, face-to-face interaction, social skills, and group processing (Johnson, Johnson & Holubec 2013). Success with cooperative learning is associated with success in each of these areas.

Positive Interdependence

Positive interdependence requires overt actions that encourage students to develop positive attitudes toward working to benefit the group. Students who display positive interdependence share resources, act as supports for each other, and acknowledge group success over the individual (Johnson, Johnson & Holubec 1998, 2013). Although there is the goal of a group assignment, there is a recognition that individual goals complement the common goal. Cooperative learning espouses shared labor and the belief that everyone has a role in the group, with no part being more important than the next. The individual's overall success is based on jointly supporting and rewarding the other group members. This way, everyone has a stake in the outcome.

Fostering a climate of positive interdependence within the learning environment requires teachers to create and monitor learning tasks to ensure that students have a sense of well-being and belonging. Successful cooperative encounters encourage students to have a favorable view of themselves as learners and awareness of where they fit within the group. Individual members must also have confidence in their ability to contribute to the academic tasks required to get the overall task accomplished (Hulse-Killacky, Killacky & Donovan 2001). This is particularly important for students with identified learning challenges who may feel overwhelmed by the curriculum's demands and traditional assessment methods. To establish positive interdependence, students need to develop a sense that there is value to what they have to offer to the group. They must believe that they can indeed fit into and be productive members of that group (Frey, Fisher & Everlove 2009).

With insights from well-known educator Linda Darling-Hammond, a helpful video considers the importance of allocating time to building a sense of belonging. Teachers in the video, entitled *Building a Belonging Classroom* (Edutopia 2019a), address the importance of community-building activities that give students opportunities to work together and engage in conversations with each other about each other's work.

Group Sharing

Activities that encourage a sense of belonging can be as simple as orchestrating students' opportunities to share opinions, beliefs, and ideas with their peers. For example, daily activities such as Circle Time (see Chap. 2) represent opportunities for students to share and exchange information. The teacher can select a topic of the day and have students share with the large circle. Alternatively, they can break into smaller circles, discuss or create pictures to represent their ideas on the topic, and then contribute when they return to the larger circle. When oral sharing is occurring informally, permitting students to "pass" is also an important safety net that some participants may need from time to time.

A video example, *60 Second Strategy*: *Community Circles* (Edutopia 2020), demonstrates the use of community circles. Students are given time to participate and practice uninterrupted sharing as they learn more about each other. During the activity, teachers emphasize the critical importance of respectful listening.

Role-Playing

Role-playing and interactive games based on games like "Pictionary" or "Charades," when played in teams, encourage students to rely on the effort that is made by each team member to give clues to help advance the team's overall ability to solve problems. Eventually, the solution evolves from the group effort. Teachers can draw themes for these interactive activities from vocabulary words or content from literature or history readings. Activities such as this allow practice for the interdependence needed by cooperative teams.

Individual Accountability

Individual accountability refers to group members' recognition that they are accountable for the individual contributions to the group. This encourages participants to become stronger and more adept at their skills, ultimately strengthening the group. Therefore, as members of the group are increasingly concerned about the learning of other participants, there is greater value in understanding how each member can support and assist the others (Johnson, Johnson, & Holubec 2013).

As groups are formed and working on projects and assignments, the teacher needs to monitor individual accountability while monitoring the group's progress.

For example, as teachers navigate to observe the group work in progress, they should randomly select a group member to ask questions about the overall project. The philosophy behind individual accountability is that regardless of which individual responds to a question, they all share responsibility for the entire project. When individual students and the group recognize that this is part of how they are assessed, they are more likely to ensure that all group members are actively participating and knowledgeable about the project. Practicing through activities that allow individuals to be aware of and knowledgeable about the focus of the entire assignment, rather than just on their designated part of the assignment, is a way to lead students toward attaining individual accountability. The following practices in the classroom align with the concept of individual accountability.

Group Recitation of a Poem or Oral Retelling of a Story

Each group member chooses and learns one verse of a short poem or section of a short story. After practicing their section individually and then with their group, group members orally share the entire poem with a larger group or the teacher. The success of the retelling depends on how the whole group performs.

Group Study with Random Checking

A group is given one body of information, for example, a list of vocabulary words or math facts to review and practice individually and as a group. The teacher calls on students randomly to obtain responses. The groups' reward rests on the success of all the individual responses.

Face-to-Face Promotive Interaction

Cooperative group work benefits when members of the group have the opportunity and time for face-to-face interactions (Johnson & Johnson 2002). The idea is that the more group members can discuss, explain, and participate in direct verbal and nonverbal interactions, the more likely they are to assist, encourage, and be accountable for each other. In a review of research on the effect of face-to-face interaction on cooperative learning, Kristiansen et al. (2019) noted that a review of 34 studies suggested that students' interpersonal behavior, past experiences, and levels of communication impact the extent of the learning that takes place. Other factors were their willingness to give and to receive help. Teachers and students need preparation to understand and maintain structures through meaningful face-to-face interactions

(Sachar & Sharan 1995). Consider the following practices which require students to engage with each other in face-to-face interactions:

Blind Drawing

Students work in pairs, with one student given a drawing and the other a piece of blank paper. The drawing is shared only with one student whose objective is to explain the drawing with sufficient details to give their partner step-by-step guidance to reproduce the drawing based only on the oral depiction provided. The video, *Communication Games—Drawing #22* (Otten 2016), provides an example of secondary school students participating in a back-to-back blind drawing activity. The successful outcome of the drawing relies on both team members working cooperatively.

Parking Lot

Each student is asked to think about and prepare a statement to share information about a chosen topic. Other students are directed to listen attentively without interruption, and if they have questions or comments, they jot them down on a note card while they listen. The note cards are figuratively held in a "parking lot" until the speaker is finished, and then the questions can be addressed by the speaker one at a time to help clarify any misunderstandings. This exercise teaches participants that cooperation also means allowing others to go first, being willing to wait for your turn, and that all participants' ideas and questions are relevant and valued.

Social Skills

Working as part of a cooperative group requires specific social skills such as communication, respect for others, and willingness to participate (Goodwin 1999). When building a cooperative climate, teachers need to help students develop and hone appropriate skills. To accomplish cooperative classroom climates, Johnson et al. (1990) note that teachers need to build some structures to support group processing since group productivity seems to increase when processing is a part of the group experience.

In the following video Darling-Hammond stresses that schools must pay attention to both social-emotional and academic learning. Skills related to interaction and self-management are required to engage in project-based learning. Students must do much social navigation to accomplish group projects. They must call on many social skill sets, and these are areas where they will need support as they learn. These social themes are addressed in the video entitled *Linda Darling-Hammond on creating a collaborative classroom* (Edutopia 2012). Some of the skills noted in the video as necessary for the development of appropriate social practices during cooperative engagements include the following:

Participation. The value of participation may need to be taught directly to students via activities and daily involvement in tasks designed to increase students' sense of belonging and importance in the class.

Respect for others. To engage appropriately, group members must feel that each member's contribution is significant. This will be especially relevant in situations with a heterogeneous mix of students, where some may have more robust capabilities than others in particular knowledge or physical skills.

Listening to and receiving information. Listening to opinions and sharing information are required to allow everyone in the workgroup to participate. Listening attentively and not interrupting are vital to cooperative work.

Turn-taking. Whether a shared task is complex or straightforward, reciprocal turn-taking is critical to ensure an exchange of information with a proper flow and logic.

Activities to Encourage Participation, Turn-Taking, and Respect-Building Skills

Message relay activities. Teachers prepare note cards with various messages. Members of a group line up and take turns giving and receiving a message one to the other. The first person quietly reads a message to the second person so only that person can hear. Once the message is received, the next person acts as the sender and passes it on to the next student. The message relay continues until it reaches the last student, who then says the message out loud. The group then discusses the final delivery of the message, paying attention to how the accuracy, meaning, and content changed during the relay. The idea is to practice listening for accuracy and transmitting the message without judgment.

Leadership assignments. Teachers assign weekly roles to teams of students. Teams can include a class monitor to set up the classroom for activities, inventory checkers to update the availability of materials, and a communication patrol to relay information between the classroom and other parts of the building. Teachers can attach a compounding reward system to these activities where teams earn rewards over time. Rewards may be tangible at first and fade to more intangible ones over time. Techniques such as this, designed to incorporate all students over time, working in teams, are more likely to encourage students to prepare for active participatory roles.

Give One, Get One. Students write as much as possible about a given topic in a set time. Students turn to their peers and give one piece of information and then receive one piece. Whenever the students receive information they did not have, they add it to their list of responses. This process repeats itself to allow students to interact through talking and listening as they share and exchange information. They are then allowed time to ponder what they agreed on and what they learned from each other.

Group Processing

Group members need time to process how their group functions, the extent of goal achievement, and how successful their working relationships are (Bertucci, Johnson, Johnson, & Conte 2012). Groups must establish and maintain an environment where all members can exchange and share ideas and receive and process others' ideas. Students need to monitor their group process to ensure that they are staying on track with the assigned task or project, keep track of what still needs to be done, and gauge how effectively members are functioning.

A video from Cornell Center for Teaching Innovation (2017) entitled *Supporting student group work* emphasizes the importance of students having guidance and structures to aid the group process. Other suggestions to improve group processes include the following:

- Groups periodically meet to monitor and gauge their performance.
- Teachers review and clarify rubrics with the students and give feedback so that group members can gauge their progress.
- Members provide feedback to each other based on either a rubric or a checklist agreed to during the establishment of group roles and responsibilities.
- Students are allowed to evaluate themselves. They can do this through a short survey that focuses on individual contributions to the group, the effectiveness of the interactions, and what learning is occurring.

Planning for Cooperative Instruction

The five key elements of cooperative learning discussed above provide a framework for teachers as they plan and monitor lessons (Johnson & Johnson 2002). Allowing cooperative learning to occur requires that teachers embrace learning experiences that may evolve and change as lessons unfold, as group projects can sometimes take on a life of their own. Developing cooperative learning environments will require flexibility, adaptability, and familiarity with students' knowledge and skills. Consideration must be given to the extent to which an assignment is appropriate for group work rather than for individual completion. An assignment or project must be sufficiently complex and interesting to engage all members of the group. Consideration must also be given to how the students' capabilities can complement each other, and the behaviors and work habits of the participants. Identifying how the group will be monitored and graded or rewarded also requires planning.

Selecting Assignments

Some helpful hints for cooperative learning lessons, adapted from Palmer et al. (2010), are outlined below:

- When introducing cooperative activities to students, start simply.
- Have students complete a task with which they are familiar and have had some success. For example, a math problem they each solve. Invite them to select a peer and explain how they solved the problem. The other students can share alternate ways they solved the same problem, exchanging information about challenges they had and so on.
- Working with a peer may remove some of the tension students feel when they must interact with larger numbers. It allows them a chance to learn and practice some of the skills required for larger cooperative endeavors.
- Start a cooperative lesson by giving information (lecture, video, or article review) and then set the students to work on the cooperative activity. In this manner, they enter the activity with some information to start their dialogue and actions.
- When beginning cooperative learning, start with one subject at a time until students gain comfort and familiarity with the process.
- Allow students some choice regarding roles and activities to which they are comfortable committing.
- At the outset, provide worksheets, guidelines, reference charts, or rubrics to which the group can refer as they navigate expectations for completing group work.
- Keep group behavior expectations posted and visible during cooperative work. Over time, and with guided practice, students will learn to develop their own visuals related to the group's rules, timelines, and expectations.

Below are some examples of the types of assignments that are appropriate for group work:

Preschool students: After a nature tour around the school's outdoor environment, students use the various flora and fauna they collect to complete a class art project. With young children, discussion and efforts to collaborate on this project may be teacher-directed through modeling and demonstration, while the children participate jointly to complete a mural.

Elementary: Students choose and read about their favorite marine animal and create a fact sheet about their selected animal. They work as a team to create a marine-themed mural using craft materials of their choosing. Students use the individual fact sheets to collaborate and work together to prepare a script used by group members, acting as tour guides, to take visitors through a gallery walk to explain the mural.

Secondary: Students select or are assigned a book to study. Each group member will read a different chapter and then share information and insights about the content with their group. Next, they combine their individual insights into a summary of all the chapters to share with their group and with other groups.

Purpose of Groups

Johnson and Johnson (1999a, b) suggest that teachers must consider the purpose of group activities when deciding what type of grouping is needed. Groups may be informal, formal, or base groups depending on the complexity of the activity.

Informal groups: Involve students working with a peer to engage in brief exchanges of information. These pairings can rotate from 1 day to the next.

Formal groups: Groups stay together for longer term assignments which may have deeper context and more in-depth expectations. Application and understanding of the five elements (*positive interdependence, individual accountability, face-to-face interaction, social skills, and group processing*), which are critical to cooperative work, need to be solidly in force for these kinds of groups to be successful.

Base groups: Groups are organized to fulfill some of the more standard requirements of the class. For example, it could be a group that has exchanged phone numbers to share class-wide information about schedules, keep each other reminded of school events, check in on each other if anyone is absent, and so on. Marzano (2001) has suggested that base groups can be formed for the entire school year. In addition to completing routine tasks in the school, they may sometimes engage in different out-of-school activities together.

Factors to Consider When Forming Groups

Cooperative grouping aligns with research that stresses heterogeneous grouping as beneficial to lower performing students academically and socially (Burris et al. 2006; Saleh et al. 2005). Groupings for cooperative activities should therefore be structured to anticipate different performance levels, and from this perspective, every student has something valuable to contribute to the learning encounters. Teachers need to be responsible for grouping rather than relying on students to group themselves so that attention is paid to balancing skill sets across the group, in order to advance students' likelihood of learning from each other and seeing the value in others' contributions.

Size of the group. Group size should be sufficiently low so that everyone has a manageable role and the group dynamic is not intimidating or overwhelming. Three to five students are the typical size, depending on the nature and complexity of the assignment.

The complexity of the task. Assignments that are multifaceted and have varying depth and scope requirements are more likely to be appropriate for group work. Bloom's taxonomy (Anderson & Krathwohl 2001) can provide information about the different process skills and expectations various assignments rely on. This can help in planning and organizing the group around expectations of the task or project.

Individual and group expectations. Knowledge about the students' behaviors and work patterns needs to be taken into account.

Depth and scope of knowledge and skills. Assignments should allow various ways for students of different abilities to demonstrate their learning. Therefore, the extent to which students have access to needed information must be considered.

When creating groups, teachers can assign roles. The video example, *60 Second-Strategy: Cooperative Learning Roles* (Edutopia 2018), depicts how random designations are made to ensure that all students participate.

Rewarding in a Cooperative Environment

Students need to understand how they will be rewarded and graded so that it becomes evident that evaluation is not just about them but is linked to the task and the group performance (Vedder & Veendrick 2003). There must be clarity about what their tasks are and what is expected of them in terms of completion, accuracy, and cooperative effort. Use of a checklist or a rubric that outlines a continuum of expected performance levels is helpful. Younger students at the early stages of writing a simple story will need to be explicitly shown what to do and have expectations explained. For example, if the expectation is to write three simple sentences and then draw a picture or vice versa—they should have a reference rubric, depicted in words and pictures, to represent their task's expectations.

Establishing Work Habits and Behaviors

Modeling of Expectations and Routines

Students will need preparation to work effectively in cooperative groups. Preparation for engaging students to work with their peers requires teachers to be aware of their students' emotional states and ways to monitor and manage these interactions to maintain students' well-being. Teachers need to embed guidance and support into the curriculum and play a critical role in developing students' self-confidence and skills needed to interact socially during cooperative tasks (Hornby & Atkinson 2003).

Behaviors appropriate to cooperative team activities need to be made explicit. Cooperative work will prove challenging in a classroom that lacks appropriate structures and management. Chapter 4 on Direct Instruction addresses the need to provide students with appropriate demonstrations before starting independent work. Preparation for cooperative work will require the same degree of instruction. Just as students must learn and follow procedures, teachers must also learn how to convey the details of procedures via their practices and their instruction (Wong 2009).

In their video entitled *Teaching Self-Regulation by Modeling* Edutopia (2019b) provides an example of a teacher modeling expectations and routines and explaining the importance of self-regulation in a cooperative environment.

Setting Norms and Clarifying Rules and Responsibilities

Setting norms or rules for cooperative practice establishes a climate and environment that welcome and accept variations in opinions and ways of functioning. Collective experiences may sometimes require students to step out of their comfort zone. Therefore, it is essential to have norms to prevent and rectify any interfering behaviors that may interrupt the students' interactions. As outlined below, establishing norms should involve the teacher brainstorming with the group to identify the appropriate actions and behaviors during any cooperative activity.

- The brainstorming process starts with asking participants to openly contribute ideas about behaviors and actions needed for productive group work to occur.
- All responses are listed and discussed as a group.
- Each item on the list is reviewed and clarified to gain a clear understanding of what it means.
- Revise the list as appropriate.
- Where there are similarities, the responses are refined or consolidated.
- Ensure group agreement to the norms.
- The agreed-upon norms are frequently revisited before cooperative work activities start.

The importance of establishing and adhering to behavior contracts is addressed in the video *Social Contracts Foster Community in the Classroom* (Edutopia 2019c). It exemplifies how teachers can establish ground rules that everyone should follow in a cooperative climate. This is reiterated by San Bernardino City Schools (2016) in their video, *Teaching procedures, rules and respect during the first days of seventh grade*, to explain the value of setting norms to establish a positive classroom environment. The importance of having a shared classroom language is discussed. It is also noted that students must consider their behaviors and be active with problem-solving around regulating their behaviors.

Making Cooperative Learning Strategies Part of Classroom Routines

Some simple cooperative learning strategies can be incorporated into classroom routines at all levels from early childhood through to tertiary education. An example of this which is very useful in a wide range of settings is "think-pair-share." This activity engages students in working cooperatively to discuss and exchange their thoughts on specific topics. Popularized by Johnson and Johnson (1991), this technique motivates students by asking them questions and giving them time to reflect before writing down their responses. The students are then paired up and allowed to exchange and discuss their responses with a partner. The paired teams then share answers with the whole class or in small groups allowing the teacher to observe and check for understanding. The video, *Think, Pair, Share*, Literacy How (2016) demonstrates how students in a primary classroom engage in an activity to explain their solutions to math addition problems. After using a whiteboard to solve the problem individually, students share their method with a partner and eventually with the whole class. In another example, *Using think, pair, share in the classroom* (Reading Rockets 2013), the teacher demonstrates the activity by conducting an oral reading of a story and asking questions which the students are then given time to think about. Following that, the students share their responses with a partner.

This technique is one that is appropriate for use across all levels, as the actions described can be applied to topics that range from simple to complex or technical. The goal is for the participants to engage and take time to process their thoughts on a topic before sharing and exploring their own understanding through listening to others.

Cooperative Learning Strategies for Elementary Students

Numbered Heads Together (Kagan 1994)

Students are grouped into four-person teams to solve problems. The team's composition should be as diverse as possible, ensuring that students of various skill levels are included. The teacher poses a question or gives a problem to the groups and provides them a specified time to work on the problem. Students then all put their heads together to discuss and work on solving the problem.

After students have had time to process the problem and develop an answer, the teacher elicits responses. The teacher randomly selects a student to provide their answer. They may call on another student from that same group to see if they agreed with the answer or want to elaborate on the response. Alternatively, they may call on a student from another group. The teacher provides feedback to acknowledge and correct responses as needed.

This method encourages face-to-face interaction with peers working on the same problem. It also allows teachers to gather the information they can utilize to determine how groups process the information and work within the group. This strategy can be used to address questions about reading material, social studies, science content, or mathematics problems. The video, *Kagan Cooperative Learning - Numbered Heads Together* (The Inspire Partnership 2015), uses this strategy to teach one aspect of mathematics in an English primary school.

Another video example from Prince William County Public Schools (2015), *Kagan Structure: Numbered Heads Together Mrs. Trachtenberg 1st Grade*, depicts how elementary students in the USA collaborate in groups of four to review historical facts.

Four Corners

Another Kagan strategy is known as four corners (Kagan 1994). This is an activity in which four locations are identified in the classroom. Each corner or location in the room represents a different answer or opinion on a topic. This activity can be conducted with young students to determine their knowledge or opinions. For example, the goal may be to identify their knowledge of different shapes or recognition of numerals. If assessing knowledge of shapes, each of the four corners is represented by a visual depiction of a different shape. The steps involved in this activity are as follows:

- The teacher calls out a shape by name and asks the students to walk to the corner that best matches what was said, e.g., circle, triangle, square, and rectangle.
- After moving to their chosen corner, students can be individually called on to share why they chose a particular corner.
- Teachers observe and assess student choices and provide additional clues to those who are uncertain about which corner to choose. If a student moves to the wrong corner, they can change their position after receiving additional clues from the teacher.
- Those who change positions are encouraged to explain what additional information or perspective made them change their corner.

Four corners can be adapted to suit different themes and topics and can be effectively conducted with small or larger groups. A video from Texas based Education Service Center Region 13 (2017), *Teacher toolkit: Four corners (Middle School)*, demonstrates how a teacher starts with an open-ended question, asking students to think about the extent to which the changing weather affects them. Students are then given time to think and individually write down their thoughts in response to the question. Next, they are asked to move to a designated section of the room where each section represents a different response to the question (a whole lot, somewhat, a little bit, not at all). Once students have selected a response area, they move to that section of the room and then share their thoughts with group members at their section. The activity concludes with students returning to their seats to share with the larger group. Several of the advantages noted by the teacher are that this cooperative activity gets students up and moving, it encourages them to engage with each other in order to participate, and it gives them an opportunity to express themselves to their peers.

Cooperative Learning Strategies for Middle and High School Students

Jigsaw (Aronson & Patnoe 1997)

The jigsaw strategy helps students learn about a significant topic by breaking it down into smaller subsections. For example, if students have multiple chapters of a book to read and review, the jigsaw process breaks information down into smaller subsections that are more manageable. Students break into threes or fours, and each group focuses on a different chapter or content to read. Individuals within the group read the section independently, share what they have learned from the chapter in their small group, and agree on relevant information within the chapter. Individuals from each group then disperse to another group, who had a different chapter, and they share and exchange the key points with the new group. This continues until all chapter information is shared. Students can use this jigsaw method to process lengthy reading material or to manage large group projects.

The video, entitled *The Jigsaw Method*, (Cult of Pedagogy 2015), outlines the steps involved in Jigsaw One and Jigsaw Two. A second video on the jigsaw strategy, *Cooperative learning: The Jigsaw method* (Reading Rockets 2012), provides an example of how to conduct jigsaw in a classroom setting. In this example, students read texts about gardening, and then they organize what they learned using graphic organizers before rotating around to other groups to share their information. The teacher concludes by returning to the large class structure to debrief and consolidate what the students have learned.

Student Teams Achievement Divisions (STAD) (Slavin 1995)

The STAD strategy rewards teams based on their improvement over time. The class divides into several teams of four or five students. The teams should represent a heterogeneous mix based on varied abilities, academic performance, ethnicities, and other features appropriate to the setting. The students complete a quiz or a task individually. Although work is graded individually, scoring is based on the extent of improvement over time. Also, the team receives the combined score of all the team members. When students engage in future learning, team members are expected to assist each other in mastering the content so that as individual scores improve, so does the team's score. The team is rewarded for its efforts according to a pre-established reward system.

The video, *Student Teams—Achievement Divisions (STAD)* (Azul 2016), provides a simple explanation and example of STAD. A second video entitled *VLOG 7: More than the distance: STAD in Athletics* (Goodyear 2015), focuses on the potential use of STAD in the teaching of physical education lessons.

Group Investigation (Sharan and Sharan 1990)

In group investigation the teacher initiates the process by identifying a topic for investigation and organizes students into research groups. The groups follow the stages outlined below to accomplish their project.

Stage one. The teacher explores the topic by exposing the students to content through lectures, media presentations, magazines, picture books, articles, guest speakers, or field trips. The students then identify subtopics for their inquiry. All the subtopics are listed and categorized by the teacher. Students are grouped according to the categories that are of interest to them.

Stage two. Students decide in their small groups which areas they will further investigate, how to proceed, and what resources they will need. Individual roles are assigned, and the group discusses how each person will contribute and be monitored.

Stage three. The students carry out the investigations. Students gather information from their sources and discuss their work with each other.

Stage four. The students prepare a final report, and the data gathering moves on to clarifying their presentation. Examples of presentations are visual displays, models, a written report, or a slideshow.

Stage five. Students present the final report.

Stage six. Evaluation: Teachers can collaborate with students to evaluate their learning.

The video, entitled *Teaching Group Work: Building Student Collaboration and Agency* (Edutopia 2016), illustrates some aspects of using the group investigation approach in a high school classroom.

Conclusion

Cooperative learning includes many of the features which experienced educators agree are effective. Working together on learning teams allows students to work in diverse groups, smaller than the entire class, which helps to set the tone for understanding and accepting differences that others bring to the learning experience. As societies worldwide are globalized, learning to be part of a group grounded in positive interdependence becomes a critical skill that many students will need in other facets of their lives. Schools and classrooms need to increase efforts to improve inclusive practices for students with varied abilities and language needs. Therefore, cooperative learning practices outlined in this chapter provide insight into ways to encourage and foster the types of exchanges that allow all students to flourish. With the student-to-teacher ratios increasing in many school settings, creating cooperative learning climates and approaches seems logical to expand students' supports and learning options.

References

Anderson, L. W., & Krathwohl, D. R. (2001). *A taxonomy for learning, teaching, and assessing: A revision of Bloom's taxonomy of educational objectives*. Longman.

Aronson, E., & Patnoe, S. (1997). *The jigsaw classroom: Building cooperation in the classroom*. Longman.

Azul, Z. (2016, April 6). *Student teams - Achievement divisions (STAD) [Video]*. YouTube. https://www.youtube.com/watch?v=NP85JtkrV3Y

Bertucci, A., Johnson, D., Johnson, R., & Conte, S. (2012). Influence of group processing on achievement and perception of social and academic support in elementary inexperienced cooperative learning groups. *Journal of Educational Research, 105*(5), 329–335.

Brown, D., & Thomson, C. (2000). *Cooperative learning in New Zealand schools*. Dunmore Press.

Burris, C. C., Heubert, J. P., & Levin, H. M. (2006). Accelerating mathematics achievement using heterogeneous grouping. *American Educational Research Journal, 43*(1), 137–154.

Cornell Center for Teaching Innovation. (2017, November 29). *Supporting student group work [Video]*. YouTube. https://www.youtube.com/watch?v=tt9pm3yeiwE

Cult of Pedagogy. (2015, April 15). *The Jigsaw method [Video]*. YouTube. https://www.youtube.com/watch?v=euhtXUgBEts

Doolittle, P. E. (1995). *Understanding cooperative learning through Vygotsky's zone of proximal development*. ERIC Clearinghouse.

Education Service Center Region13. (2017, December 11). *Teacher toolkit: Four corners (middle school) [Video]*. YouTube. https://www.youtube.com/watch?v=M2XmJQ9FL5A

Edutopia. (2012, March 15). *Linda Darling-Hammond on creating a collaborative classroom [Video]*. YouTube. https://www.youtube.com/watch?v=giYs1r9Lqwo

Edutopia. (2016, May 12). *Teaching group work: Building student collaboration and agency [Video]*. YouTube. https://www.youtube.com/watch?v=-Mb9-At2Ss0

Edutopia. (2018, November 2). *60 second-strategy: Cooperative learning roles [Video]*. YouTube. https://www.youtube.com/watch?v=zR6rTKPkjgQ

Edutopia. (2019a, February 28). *Building a belonging classroom [Video]*. YouTube. https://www.youtube.com/watch?v=Q6niuYToam4

Edutopia. (2019b, January 14). *Teaching Self-Regulation by Modeling [Video]*. YouTube. https://www.youtube.com/watch?v=UD9m5n-ZpB0

Edutopia. (2019c, October 3). *Social contracts foster community in the classroom [Video]*. YouTube. https://www.youtube.com/watch?v=OjzweCyJIok

Edutopia. (2020, February 21). *60 second-strategy: Community circles [Video]*. YouTube. https://www.youtube.com/watch?v=1fuLSU3bE-w

Frey, N., Fisher, D., & Everlove, S. (2009). *Productive group work: How to engage students, build teamwork, and promote understanding*. ASCD.

Gillies, R. (2016). Cooperative learning: Review of research and practice. *Australian Journal of Teacher Education, 41*(3), 39–54.

Goodyear, V. (2015, April 16). *VLOG 7: More than the distance: STAD in athletics [Video]*. YouTube. https://www.youtube.com/watch?v=gP3zL5TjW0E

Goodwin, M. (1999). Cooperative learning and social skills: What skills to teach and how to teach them. *Intervention in School and Clinic, 35*(1), 29–33.

Hattie, J. (2009). *Visible learning: A synthesis of over 800 meta-analyses related to achievement.* Routledge.

Hattie, J. (2012). *Visible learning for teachers: Maximizing impact on learning.* Routledge.

Hornby, G. (2009). The effectiveness of cooperative learning with trainee teachers. *Journal of Education for Teaching, 35*(2), 161–168.

Hornby, G., & Atkinson, M. (2003). A framework for promoting mental health in school. *Pastoral Care in Education, 21,* 3–9.

Hulse-Killacky, D., Killacky, J., & Donigian, J. (2001). *Making task groups work in your world.* Merrill Prentice-Hall.

Johnson, D. W., & Johnson, R. T. (1991). *Learning together and alone: Cooperative, competitive, and individualistic* (3rd ed.). Prentice-Hall.

Johnson, D. W., & Johnson, R. T. (1999a). *Learning together and alone. Cooperative, competitive, and individualistic learning* (5th ed.). Allyn & Bacon.

Johnson, D. W., & Johnson, R. T. (1999b). Making cooperative learning work. *Theory Into Practice, 38*(2), 67–73.

Johnson, D. W., & Johnson, R. T. (2002). Learning together and alone: Overview and meta-analysis. *Asia Pacific Journal of Education, 22*(1), 95–105.

Johnson, D., Johnson, R., & Holubec, E. (1998). *Cooperation in the classroom.* Allyn and Bacon.

Johnson, D. W., Johnson, R., & Holubec, E. (2013). *Cooperation in the classroom* (9th ed.). Interaction.

Johnson, D., Johnson, R., Ortiz, A., & Stanne, M. (1991). The impact of positive goal and resource interdependence on achievement, interaction, and attitudes. *The Journal of General Psychology, 118*(4), 341–347.

Johnson, D., Johnson, R., Stanne, M., & Garibaldi, A. (1990). Impact of group processing on achievement in cooperative groups. *Journal of Social Psychology, 130,* 507–516.

Kagan, S. (1994). *Cooperative learning.* Resources for Teachers.

Kagan Video. (2009, September 23). *Kagan cooperative learning-structures for success part 1 [Video].* YouTube. https://www.youtube.com/watch?v=S0s_qxJDuas

Kristiansen, S., Bruner, T., Johnsen, B., & Yates, G. (2019). Face to face promotive interaction leading to successful cooperative learning: A review study. *Cogent Education, 6,* 1.

Kyndt, E., Raes, E., Lismont, B., Timmers, F., Cascallar, E., & Dochy, F. (2013). A meta-analysis of the effects of face-to-face cooperative learning. Do recent studies falsify or verify earlier findings? *Educational Research Review, 10,* 133–149.

Learning for Justice. (2012, March 15). *Basics of cooperative learning [Video].* YouTube. https://www.youtube.com/watch?v=OPc2mYftBDA

Lewin, K. (1947). Frontiers in group dynamics: Concept, method and reality in social science; social equilibria and social change. *Human Relations, 1*(1), 5–41.

Literacy How. (2016, December 7). *Think, pair, share [Video].* YouTube. https://www.youtube.com/watch?v=tPSfolz_700

Marzano, R. J. (2001). *Classroom instruction that works: Research-based strategies for increasing student achievement.* Association for Supervision and Curriculum Development.

Ning, H., & Hornby, G. (2010). The effectiveness of cooperative learning in teaching English to Chinese tertiary learners. *Effective Education, 2*(2), 99–116.

Otten, H. (2016, November 29). *Communication games - Drawing *22 [Video].* YouTube. https://www.youtube.com/watch?v=8yGhNwDMT-g

Palmer, G., Peters, R., & Streetman, R. (2010). Cooperative learning. In M. Orey (Ed.), *Emerging perspectives on learning, teaching, and technology, global text.* Retrieved from https://textbookequity.org/Textbooks/Orey_Emerging_Perspectives_Learning.pdf

Prince William County Public Schools. (2015, January 30). *Kagan Structure: Numbered Heads Together Mrs. Trachtenberg 1st Grade [Video].* YouTube. https://www.youtube.com/watch?v=jqs61UX1bUw

Reading Rockets. (2012, February 16). *Cooperative learning: The jigsaw method [Video].* YouTube. https://www.youtube.com/watch?v=mtm5_w6JthA

Reading Rockets. (2013, January 29). *Using think-pair-share in the classroom [Video]*. YouTube. https://www.youtube.com/watch?v=-9AWNl-A-34

Sachar, H., & Sharan, S. (1995). Cooperative learning in the heterogeneous Israeli classroom. *International Journal of Educational Research, 23*(3), 283–292.

Saleh, M., Lazonder, A. W., & De Jong, T. (2005). Effects of within-class ability grouping on social interaction, achievement, and motivation. *Instructional Science, 33*, 105–119.

San Bernardino City Schools. (2016, September 6). *Teaching procedures, rules, and respect during the first days of seventh grade [Video]*. YouTube. https://www.youtube.com/watch?v=k7GzWs0nJig.

Sharan, Y., & Sharan, S. (1990). Group investigation expands cooperative learning. *Educational Leadership, 47*, 17–21.

Slavin, R. E. (1995). *Cooperative learning: Theory, research, and practice*. Allyn & Bacon.

The Inspire Partnership. (2015, December 7). *Kagan cooperative learning - Numbered heads together [Video]*. YouTube. https://www.youtube.com/watch?v=ARL6p1JtIuQ.

Vedder, P., & Veendrick, A. (2003). The role of the task and reward structure in cooperative learning. *Scandinavian Journal of Educational Research, 47*(5), 529–542.

Wong, H. K., Wong, R. T., & Seroyer, C. (2009). *The first days of school: How to be an effective teacher*. Harry K. Wong.

Chapter 6
Peer Tutoring

Abstract Peer tutoring provides opportunities for students to work with a peer partner to engage in roles where one serves as the tutor and the other the tutee. This chapter outlines peer tutoring as a strategy that can enable students to benefit from each other's knowledge and skill sets. A variety of methods to prepare and engage students in reciprocal peer tutoring activities are discussed. Guidelines are provided to assist teachers in establishing support structures and identifying learning outcomes appropriate to effective peer tutoring interactions. Several peer tutoring strategies suitable for different school levels are shared. When students are guided to work in partnership, helping each other organize and process information, their opportunities for improved learning are increased.

Rationale

The *Teaching and Learning Toolkit* (Education Endowment Foundation 2021) reports that peer tutoring has a moderate impact for a very low cost based on extensive evidence. Hattie's *summary of meta-analyses of studies* on the influence of peer tutoring on students' academic performance reports that it has an overall positive effect size of 0.51. Therefore, peer tutoring is considered to be an evidence-based teaching strategy. In addition, peer tutoring interactions are found to yield positive effects on both the tutor and the tutee (Hattie & Zierer 2017). Therefore, extending students' instructional encounters beyond their teacher's expertise can play a significant role in expanding student learning. Such practices reinforce and strengthen their skills and their content knowledge (Bargh & Schul 1980; Cohen et al. 1982; Fiorella & Mayer 2013). Allowing students to engage in peer tutoring supports their learning by allowing them time to review and develop their understanding as they share their knowledge and skills.

G. Hornby, D. Greaves, *Essential Evidence-Based Teaching Strategies*,
https://doi.org/10.1007/978-3-030-96229-6_6

Theory

Research on peer tutoring at the elementary and secondary school levels indicates that students receive significant academic benefits in reading and math when their involvement in such pairings is encouraged and supported (Fuchs et al. 1997). It serves as an opportunity for review and a shared learning experience in which both partners can develop the trust and interdependence needed for successful cooperative exchanges (Conrad 1974; Johnson & Johnson 2014). As noted in Chap. 5 on cooperative learning, positive peer interactions are also a means toward building mutual relationships. Learners collaborate as they are guided toward taking responsibility for their learning and building confidence as they proceed (Cohen et al. 1982). When set up as a structured activity where teachers provide oversight and foster an appropriate climate that encourages respectful and substantive engagement, learning partners are more likely to engage in meaningful practices and dialogue around learning content and processes. Students generally have positive attitudes toward peer tutoring and tend to have a more positive response when allowed to share in the tutor's role (Eiserman 1988; Facey-Shaw et al. 2005). The video entitled *Peer Tutoring: StrategyTube Video* (Deanna 2013) introduces peer tutoring, its definition, underpinning theory, practical implementation, and research on its impact on students' learning.

Peer Tutoring Models

Peer tutoring is practiced through a variety of models. These include one-directional and cross-age models in which one student serves primarily as the tutor and teaches and monitors the progress of the other. Other models encourage two students to engage in interdependence with each peer taking turns influencing the other toward some educational goal. The interdependent models include reciprocal peer tutoring, class-wide peer tutoring, and peer-assisted learning (Fuchs et al. 1997). These interdependent models involve strategies that partner similarly aged students in turn-taking learning exchanges. They are cooperative in nature with each learning from the other as they interact to fulfill different roles during these exchanges.

Planning for Peer Tutoring

Falchikov (2001) suggests that several aspects need to be considered for effective peer tutoring to occur. Among the recommendations are the following:

There must be clear criteria for functioning and an expected outcome that is very explicit. When planning for sessions, teachers and students must be clear on what students must know and do. The content, methods, and teaching tools must be available and familiar to students, who should indicate what they will be attempting to learn or demonstrate by the end of the session(s). The video, entitled *Using Reciprocal Teaching to Engage 3rd Grade Readers* (San Bernardino City Schools 2019), outlines how student roles are identified in a small group reciprocal teaching experience designed to help students with reading comprehension skills. In the example, each student is assigned roles as predictor, questioner, summarizer, and clarifier. Students read paragraphs as a group and use a guideline provided by the teacher to help them navigate the peer tutoring component of this process. Students are taught the expectations and purpose of their various roles and to conduct tasks associated with their roles. An assigned student serves as the tutor to guide the peer group through the tutoring session's expectations, keep the students on task, and involve participants as they read and discuss the passages. More details about reciprocal teaching are provided in Chap. 7.

Students should play an active part in the learning process. Students need to take turns and have opportunities to serve as both tutors and tutees. There will arguably be times when the pairing of students is such that one student has more advanced skills than another. Planning should involve including a variety of tutoring materials that allow for different types of instruction and responses. For example, if peer tutoring is being used to clarify and review a math sequence such as division, a tutor who is more adept at the skill may guide the other student through the steps. The tutor should provide objects and demonstrate and show the tutee how to distribute or divide objects into equal sets. The tutor should further observe and support the tutee as they attempt to correct their errors. The task may involve the tutor guiding the tutee through the steps with a visual sequence of the problem, and then allowing them to complete a similar problem, step-by-step, as they use the visual sequence to check their progress. The tutor and tutee may then use a calculator to check the final answer. Responses may be verbal, written, demonstrated through selecting from a series of response cards/picture cards, or through a nonverbal action such as pointing to select a response. Examples of active participation for both the tutor and the tutee are provided in Fig. 6.1: Examples of tutor and tutee actions. The figure depicts the actions that both participants should engage in, so that they get the most out of their time spent together.

Activities and work products resulting from student interactions are used for formative rather than summative purposes. Teachers should use peer tutoring to address content and skills that have already been introduced and for which there has already been teacher instruction and intervention. Work produced during these exchanges should not be used for grading but should be used for monitoring progress, giving feedback to the pairs of students, and making appropriate decisions about the future teaching needs of the students. Students can also provide feedback to each other about the progress made during peer tutoring sessions. Using the acronym SPARK, Gardner (2019) provides a useful method for teaching students to give peer feedback. He suggests the following framework for students to follow when giving practical feedback to each other:

Specific: Make sure that comments are about a specific item or section of the work.
Prescriptive: Provide a solution or strategy to improve the work.

Examples of Tutor Actions	Examples of Tutee Actions
Assist with reading sentences/passages when needed	Attempt to read sentences/passages independently
Ask questions to encourage thinking	Ask questions
Listen attentively to responses	Listen attentively to guidance that is provided
Show and explain examples	Respond and explain responses
Model actions/tasks	Follow actions/tasks that are demonstrated
Review information	Review information
Clarify information	Seek clarification of information
Restate information	Ask for additional explanation
Present a variety of examples	Ask for information to be restated
Encourage responses	Ask for examples if needed
Affirm appropriate responses	Give examples to demonstrate understanding
Express appreciation for effort made	Respond willingly
Present accurate information	Seek confirmation about responses
Display a respectful demeanour	Try even if uncertain
Allow time for responses	Be receptive to guidance
	Display a respectful demeanour
	Take time to respond

Fig. 6.1   Examples of tutor and tutee actions

Actionable: Provide feedback to provide a clear explanation of what and how
    needed changes should occur.
Referenced: Make sure that the feedback aligns with the criteria of the tasks or the
    skills being targeted.
Kind: Frame comments in a kind and supportive manner.

In the video entitled *High school: Modeling and practicing peer feedback* (Core Collaborative 2018), students are encouraged to practice giving feedback to each other about the content and quality of a written assignment. Students are provided with a *Ladder of Feedback* guideline to assess the assignment's content and clarity and to offer suggestions to strengthen the paper. In the video example, the protocol provided demonstrates how to associate the feedback with the task criteria. Students are encouraged to give each other specific suggestions and action steps to help them identify ways to improve their work.

Building Effective Peer Tutoring Teams

Attention must be paid to establishing student pairings around trust, a sense of shared purpose, and mutual respect. Another critical part of this equation is the importance of ensuring that the information disseminated and shared during a peer tutoring experience is accurate and aligned with the expectations for learning as outlined in the curriculum. Teachers must also ensure an appropriate level of instruction suitable to peer participants during the peer tutoring sessions. Students should have clarity about how to go about the process, what they need to know, and what they will do during the interaction. Monitoring these steps and providing feedback to students make these encounters more productive.

Creating an Appropriate Climate of Sharing

For students to work effectively together, there must be a sense that each has a comfort level with the other. Peer tutoring situations are frequently ones where there may not be an equal balance of knowledge and skills at the outset of interaction. Therefore, it is essential for all participants to feel that they have something to offer to peer tutoring. If there is a clear difference in skills, there must be a level of respect, each for the other, in which healthy interactions can occur. A video from Edutopia (2019) entitled *Creating a positive learning environment* demonstrates how an elementary setting works to create a welcoming environment that caters to the emotional needs of students. The goal is to develop relationships where students feel safe, emotionally grounded, and willing to trust and interact with each other.

Establishing Learning Structures to Improve Knowledge and Accuracy

Instruction appropriate to peer tutoring interactions such as content, skills to be developed, instructional adaptation, and differentiation are all areas that must be considered when planning for peer tutoring experiences. Students must be provided with appropriate tools to help them go about the process. Tools may include flash cards, reference charts and pictures, objects for demonstration, or interactive computer programs. Teachers should also role-play with students to give them guidance, and students can role-play with each other to practice actions and expectations.

Identifying Learning Outcomes

Teams that work together must have a clear outline of exactly what information they are trying to impart to each other. They should be aware of what skills it will take to impart that information and what activities to engage in as they try to present that information to each other. The outcomes for the time spent interacting must be clear so the students know what they will need to accomplish from the outset. Examples of specific outcomes would be the following:

- At the end of the session, the tutee will restate three facts from a reading passage.
- The tutee will solve three problems, two of which involve addition with regrouping and one which does not.
- The tutee will draw a sequence chart or complete the missing sections to demonstrate the steps for solving a science experiment.

Clarifying Tutoring Methods

Once the objective is clear, students need to be aware of and comfortable using tutoring methods to accomplish the desired outcome. For example, they may be provided with a video to observe, a passage to conduct a read-aloud, an audio recording to listen to, or a visual example that scripts out a sequence of events. These are examples of learning aids that can help students access and impart the information and content they need to teach to each other. The next important step is for the students to have a process to follow. Examples include providing the tutor with an instructional script that identifies the sequence of events they should follow or providing a series of questions which they will ask their tutees in order to gauge their understanding. In effect, students who serve as tutors require plans to guide the experience to make it productive for both them and the tutee.

Monitoring Progress and Providing Feedback

It is essential to ensure that the knowledge and skills students teach to the other fall within their range of ability and understanding. Therefore, teachers and instructors need to set aside time to observe and interact with the various peer groups to ensure that the foundational knowledge and skills are present. Teachers should prepare students by conducting collaborative conferences with individual students or peer partners before and after the peer tutoring experience. This approach helps assess the strength of their skills and their readiness to engage in the peer tutoring experience.

Peer tutoring sessions need periodic monitoring to ensure that the sessions are productive for both the tutor and tutee. Teachers can monitor the sessions through informal observations as peers are working together on a particular task. Such observations can be documented using a checklist or a rubric designed to outline the academic and behavioral expectations of the tutor and tutee. The actions described in Fig. 6.1 can also be used to provide elements from which teachers can select features to include on an observation checklist. Checklists need not be lengthy and can be crafted to address three or four things that the assignment requires. Teachers may use such checklists or observation protocols as they walk around to observe different peer tutoring sessions in progress. Teachers should periodically share these observations with the peer partners, with recommendations for improvement. As noted throughout previous chapters, it is also crucial for teachers to model and guide students to gather and share informative feedback about their experiences and their learning during the peer tutoring interactions. Teachers should follow up by conferencing with peer tutoring teams to help them disseminate, clarify, and utilize the feedback to improve or fill any gaps in knowledge, skills, or behaviors that still need to be addressed.

The video entitled *Teacher moderation student/teacher conferences* (Knatim 2008) demonstrates a teacher conducting one-on-one conferences with students to provide them with feedback about their writing. These interactions support students with information about how to receive feedback for improvement. These are opportunities for teachers to model the interactions that students can apply to their interactions with peers during tutoring sessions.

Peer Tutoring Strategies for Elementary Students

Class-Wide Peer Tutoring

Class-wide peer tutoring increases students' response opportunities. In many classroom environments, especially those which include diverse learning populations, making sure that all students have a chance to engage and to be involved is critical (Delquadri et al. 1986). This method also allows students to take turns as they supervise and help their classmates with responses. Class-wide peer tutoring increases opportunities for students to receive practice as well as instructional time from their peers. The steps involved in class-wide peer tutoring are as follows:

- The students are partnered into peer tutoring teams, and each pair is then further assigned to a larger team.
- A timer is used to signal the beginning of 10 min.
- The tutee is given a task to complete. This could be reading a passage, reading sentences, or completing a problem.
- After the tutee reads the passage or sentence, the tutor then asks a question. If the response is correct, the tutee may gain 2 points. If incorrect, the tutor provides the correct answer and allows the tutee to record and restate the correct answer. The tutee gains 1 point for doing this.
- After several responses, the points gained are tallied and incorporated into the group's overall score.
- The process continues again with the tutor and tutee switching roles.
- At the end of the designated time, the total points earned by the larger team are tallied.
- Teachers record these points and reward teams appropriately.

Teachers need to rotate the participants on teams to allow them to work with different students. This maintains neutrality, avoiding the likelihood of a particular group of students being identified as stronger or weaker than the others. A video from Drollinger (2015) entitled *Class-wide peer tutoring* provides an animated depiction to outline an example of the application of this strategy.

Reciprocal Peer Tutoring

Reciprocal peer tutoring is a cooperative strategy that puts students in teams to help and support each other in attaining knowledge and skills (Fantuzzo, Dimeff & Fox 1989). It is most effective when the teacher presents a detailed checklist or guidelines for conducting the activity. A demonstration by the teacher followed by time for the peer tutoring teams to practice their responsibilities is critical to its success. Students can use prepared flash cards or information sheets to engage in reciprocal review of math facts and sequences, science data, or information related to social studies and history. One way to accomplish such review is as follows:

- Individuals take turns reviewing flash cards or information sheets independently.
- They may further review by taking turns reading the cards/sheets to each other.
- After reviewing, each partner may take a turn sharing one piece of information or the facts that they recall from the review.
- The partners then take turns quizzing each other about the content on the cards/sheets.

Often, the requirement may go beyond the recall of facts to soliciting opinions. In that case, the exchange can occur similarly with the tutor recording the statement of the tutee, followed by the pair verbally sharing and comparing their opinions and explaining their rationale to each other. When pairing students, the teacher needs to plan for the different ability levels of the students, especially if more advanced reading, skills are needed. In that case, students are partnered so that at least one or the other will have a reasonable expectation of reading most of the information, even if it is a challenge for the other. The video entitled *The Reciprocal Learning Strategy* (Cult of Pedagogy 2014) provides an explanation and example of using reciprocal peer tutoring.

Peer Tutoring Strategies for Secondary Students

Peer-Assisted Learning Strategies (PALS)

Peer-assisted learning strategies (Fuchs et al. 1997) focus on peer partners working together on specific skills associated with reading and math. Initially addressing skills in the elementary grades, the developers of PALS extended the strategies to include older students with appropriate adaptations to content and skills. When applied to reading, PALS focuses on partners reading aloud, summarizing paragraphs to determine the main idea, making predictions, and reading to confirm or deny. Focus is also placed on having peer partners assist each other through feedback and make corrections for self-improvement. PALS follows the following sequence:

- Partners each take a turn reading aloud to each other for 5 min. After each has had their turn reading the passage, the partners orally retell the story. Appropriate retelling includes identification of the main characters, events, and time frames of the story. The oral retelling of the main idea should be accomplished in approximately ten words.
- Peers then state what they consider the most important thing(s) they learned from the reading passage.
- The next phase is the prediction relay stage. Before reading the next passage, each partner predicts what they think will happen next, and then reads the paragraph to test their prediction for accuracy.
- The peer partners take turns repeating this cycle until they have read through the assigned passages.

During the read-aloud phase, the tutor assists the tutee with correcting mispronunciations, decoding words, and word meanings. The tutor uses demonstration to encourage the tutee to sound out the word. Eventually if the tutee is unable to do so the tutor reads the word to them. In their video, *PALS High School: Partner reading*, The IRIS Center Video Collection (2018) demonstrates how peers assist each other with word decoding and actively listen as their partner retells what they have read.

Peer Editing

Students can also partner in peer tutoring teams to review and offer corrective feedback for improving writing assignments. During the editing process, the peer partners follow a sequence in which they exchange each other's writing assignments and provide feedback via a three-step process which involves the tutor first complimenting, and then suggesting, followed by the tutee correcting the work based on the suggestions given.

- After reading and reflecting on their partner's work, the tutor starts by providing the tutee with a compliment about the work. Compliments focus on what the reader found interesting and generally liked about the written piece. Compliments can range from an appreciation for the handwriting style to ways in which the work demonstrated clarity of ideas, expression, intrigue, or writing style, to mention a few. Compliments can be written down or verbally shared with the tutee. Compliments should be positive and should connect to something specific which the reader enjoyed.
- Next, the tutor provides suggestions for improvement while still maintaining a positive attitude and wording. Recommendations may include offering alterna-

tive vocabulary or sentence structure to improve clarity and expression or adding more information to give the story greater detail.

- The tutee then follows up by revisiting their writing assignments and making changes based on the feedback received.

The video from Amorella (2014) on *Peer Editing* provides an example of the sequence outlined above.

Conclusion

Including all students in the learning process is critical to establishing classroom climates founded on equity. Therefore, building strong and productive interpersonal relationships between classmates must be a focal point of learning. Like cooperative learning, peer tutoring places the student at the center of the learning process in learning situations that are both social and academic. This approach encourages active participation, which can be readily adapted to the capabilities of different students and aligns well with inclusive classroom practices. As a method that relies on students' ability to develop relationships and engage in meaningful reciprocal learning exchanges, peer tutoring has proven to be an extremely useful evidence-based strategy.

References

Amorella, M. (2014, January 29). *Peer editing [Video]*. YouTube. https://www.youtube.com/watch?v=0FqkkW2t1SY&feature=youtu.be

Bargh, J. A., & Schul, Y. (1980). On the cognitive benefits of teaching. *Journal of Educational Psychology, 72*(5), 593–604.

Cohen, P. A., Kulik, J. A., & Kulik, C. (1982). Educational outcomes of tutoring: A meta-analysis of findings. *American Educational Research Journal, 19*(2), 237–248.

Conrad, E. (1974). *Peer tutoring: A cooperative learning experience*. Arizona Center for Educational Research and Development.

Core Collaborative. (2018, January 28). *High school: Modeling and practicing peer feedback [Video]*. YouTube. https://www.youtube.com/watch?v=GvHsmnJLYr4

Cult of Pedagogy. (2014, February 28). *The reciprocal learning strategy [Video]*. YouTube. https://www.youtube.com/watch?v=_-3Kw1ildCc

Deanna, B. (2013, February 3). *Peer tutoring: Strategy tube video [Video]*. YouTube. https://www.youtube.com/watch?v=k9O4uSIQoiM

Delquadri, J., Greenwood, C., Whorton, D. M., Carta, J., & Hall, R. (1986). Classwide peer tutoring. *Exceptional Children, 52*, 535–542.

Drollinger, M. (2015, October 12). *Class wide peer tutoring [Video]*. YouTube. https://www.youtube.com/watch?v=V9i5yWzz79s

Education Endowment Foundation. (2021, October 28). *Teaching and learning toolkit*. EEF. https://educationendowmentfoundation.org.uk/education-evidence/teaching-learning-toolkit

Edutopia. (2019, January 14). *Creating a positive learning environment [Video]*. YouTube. https://www.youtube.com/watch?v=T9ynlPs_NTM

Eiserman, W. D. (1988). Three types of peer tutoring: Effects on the attitudes of students with learning disabilities and their regular class peers. *Journal of Learning Disabilities, 21*(4), 249–252.

Facey-Shaw, L., & Golding, P. (2005). Effects of peer tutoring and attitude on academic performance of first year introductory programming students. *Proceedings Frontiers in Education 35th Annual Conference*, S1E-S1E.

Falchikov, N. (2001). *Learning together: Peer tutoring in higher education*. Routledge Falmer.

Fantuzzo, J. W., Riggio, R. E., Connelly, S., & Dimeff, L. A. (1989). Effects of reciprocal peer tutoring on academic achievement and psychological adjustment: A component analysis. *Journal of Educational Psychology, 81*(2), 173–177.

Fiorella, L., & Mayer, R. E. (2013). The relative benefits of learning by teaching and teaching expectancy. *Contemporary Educational Psychology, 38*(4), 281–288.

Fuchs, D., Fuchs, L., Mathes, P., & Simmons, D. (1997). Peer-assisted learning strategies: Making classrooms more responsive to diversity. *American Educational Research Journal, 34*(1), 174–206.

Gardner, M. (2019). Teaching students to give peer feedback. Retrieved from https://www.edutopia.org/article/teaching-students-give-peer-feedback.

Hattie, J., & Zierer, K. (2017). *10 Mindframes for visible learning: Teaching for success* (1st ed.). Routledge.

Johnson, D. W., & Johnson, R. T. (2014). Cooperative learning in 21st century. *Anales de Psicología, 30*(3), 841–851.

Knatim. (2008, February 16). *Teacher moderation student/teacher conferences [Video]*. YouTube. https://www.youtube.com/watch?v=Pad1eAcsHho&feature=youtu.be

San Bernardino City Schools. (2019, April 1). *Using reciprocal teaching to engage 3rd grade readers [Video]*. YouTube. https://www.youtube.com/watch?v=tC032EkLC3A

The IRIS Center Video Collection. (2018, May 4). *PALS high school: Partner reading with retell [Video]*. YouTube. https://www.youtube.com/watch?v=fpwIC7z1uXE

Chapter 7
Metacognitive Strategies

Abstract This chapter promotes teachers' use of metacognitive strategies to help students reflect on how to improve their learning. It also provides insight into the research and theory behind metacognitive learning strategies and presents specific strategies which are useful for helping students improve their overall study skills. When students have metacognitive awareness, they can reflect on the practices and processes they use to help them understand information and solve problems. In so doing, students can more easily assess and improve their performance and plan the additional work needed to accomplish their learning goals.

Rationale

Metacognitive strategies are techniques used to help students understand the way they learn and do this more effectively. The *Teaching and Learning Toolkit* (Education Endowment Foundation 2021) reports that metacognitive strategies have a high impact based on extensive evidence. In *Hattie's 2015 online update* the overall average effect size for metacognitive strategies is reported to be 0.60. This is an above-average effect size for educational interventions, clearly demonstrating its potential for improving the levels of academic achievement, and placing it among some of the most effective interventions that teachers can use. Metacognitive strategy training involves explicitly teaching and coaching students in the thinking skills that will allow them to improve their learning. The recommendations discussed in this chapter aim to increase teachers' knowledge in the use of metacognitive strategies and assist them at being more adept at instructing students to take greater control of their learning.

Theory

Research on understanding cognition in early learners evolved out of work pioneered by Jean Piaget, who identified specific stages of child development, during which particular skill sets and cognitive abilities developed. One of the stages he identified is the formal operations stage when, around the age of 12 years, children were considered to develop the ability to think about their cognitive processing and their way of learning. Further research by Flavell (1976) considered metacognition as the interconnection between how individuals monitor, regulate, and orchestrate their thinking processes to attain a particular goal. Terminology that is often associated with metacognition includes metacognitive awareness, self-awareness, self-regulation, and self-reflection (Pintrich 2002). Teachers who teach using metacognitive strategies can positively influence students by helping them to acquire new information and skills more efficiently (McLeskey, Rosenberg & Westling 2013). Therefore, teachers should aim to apply these strategies to heighten students' self-awareness in order to help them develop effective study skills.

Study Skills

The teaching of study skills typically focuses on learning skills such as time and resource management, questioning, note-taking, summarizing, organization, using checklists, and learning various strategies for improving memory such as rehearsal and mnemonics (Mitchell & Sutherland 2020). The video entitled *How to Study Effectively for School or College [Top 6 Science-Based Study Skills]* from Memorize Academy 2016) suggests strategies for organizing and studying new information, including switching from one topic to the next to look for connections; asking questions as new knowledge is presented while trying to explain it relative to already known information; and trying to identify concrete examples to explain new situations. All these actions encourage student self-reflection about how they process and complete tasks. There are many other useful strategies with similar aims, and several of the most extensively researched metacognitive strategies that can be implemented in classrooms with students of various ages are outlined below.

Concept Mapping

Concept mapping is a strategy that can be applied in all curriculum areas to demonstrate the relationships between ideas. It is a strategy that helps students recall information, present ideas, and organize thoughts. Other terms for concept mapping are "semantic mapping" and "graphic organizers" (McLeskey et al. 2013). Since these strategies build on prior knowledge and are active forms of learning, they can be effective teaching tools. The use of these interventions has been found by Hattie to have an overall effect size of 0.64 showing that they are highly effective in improving academic achievement.

Concept mapping is beneficial at the start of a lesson to set out the concepts and vocabulary involved in the subject to be taught. A video from Lucidchart (2018) entitled *How to make a concept map*, demonstrates how a teacher develops a concept map by first starting with the central concept, in this case, the solar system. She then brainstorms with the class to come up with terms associated with solar systems, such as the moon, sun, planets, Jupiter, and Pluto. The relationships between the main concept and associated concepts are then established by drawing a diagram to categorize and link the concepts. Additional concepts and relationships are gathered and discussed for inclusion into the diagram. This method portrays the components of the solar system using a visual representation of information that is designed to encourage thinking while also creating a tool to support understanding.

Mnemonics

The use of mnemonics dates back to ancient Greece when they were used to recall large quantities of unusual information that would be difficult to remember. Modern research on this strategy suggests that keywords, acronyms, rhymes, songs, or stories with visual imagery all support students' learning (Putnam 2015; Scruggs & Mastropieri 2000). The use of such interventions has been found by Hattie to have an overall effect size of 0.80 showing that they are highly effective in improving academic achievement.

A mnemonic is an instructional strategy designed to help students improve their memory of important information. This technique connects new learning to prior knowledge using visual and acoustic cues. The basic types of mnemonic strategies rely on the use of keywords, rhyming words, or acronyms. One common acronym is "Richard Of York Gained Battle In Vain." This acronym aids the recall of the primary colors red, orange, yellow, green, blue, indigo, and violet. Similarly, to recall the names of the five Great Lakes in North America, the acronym **HOMES** helps to remember the lakes: Huron, Ontario, Michigan, Erie, and Superior. A verse to recall information about the number of days in each calendar month is as follows: 30 days has September, April, June, and November. All the rest have 31, except February, which has 28 days each year and 29 days in a leap year.

The use of keywords is perhaps one of the more common mnemonic methods for helping students learn new vocabulary. This method requires students to associate a visual representation with a keyword and recall the meaning of that word through recollection of the visual imagery. The following outline suggests the steps that a teacher may follow to help students learn a specific word using this technique:

Record: First, the teacher records a word that will be familiar to the student and connects it to the new vocabulary word. For example, the new vocabulary word may be "antique," defined as an item that is very valuable because of its age. The keyword is "ant."

Relate: Next, the teacher assists students with relating the keyword to the new word. To accomplish this, the teacher and class may come up with a picture of an ant who looks very old, but it is wearing a crown of gold and standing on a pile of gold coins. Discussing what the picture depicts about the new vocabulary word helps connect the image to the new word and serves as the retrieval path for recalling the new word's meaning.

Practice: Students need time to practice, and direct guidance as they develop confidence with this process.

The video, entitled *Powerful Mnemonic Techniques* from Tiny Medicine (2020), provides further examples of how to most effectively use mnemonics to optimize learning.

SQ3R Reading Method

SQ3R, invented by Francis Robinson (1946), is beneficial for reviewing informational text, where there are large amounts of information to be processed. Many school textbooks in history, social studies, and science contain large bodies of knowledge, which, if broken down and considered one section at a time, will improve the understanding of student readers. This technique is equally applicable whether the text is at a more straightforward reading level or a more advanced reading level. The steps in the process are as follows:

1. *Survey*. Before beginning a new chapter, skim the material and get a feel for the main topics and ideas in the text. When surveying and scanning the text, readers should be encouraged to look for keywords and explore the pictures or figures associated with each section of the text. It is also helpful to encourage students to read each paragraph's introductory and closing sentences. These actions help students develop a preliminary idea about the chapter's content.
2. *Question*. Use questions to guide the reading. When students develop inquiries related to the anticipated content, it helps them set a goal for their reading. Reading then serves the purpose of gathering information to help them answer a specific question. For example, suppose the title of a section is "Unusual rock formations across the world." In that case, it is helpful for a reader to frame questions such as "what do unusual rock formations look like" or "what countries in the world have unusual rock formations."
3. *Read*. While reading, look for answers to the questions. As solutions and other pertinent information are identified, students should be encouraged to make notes in the margins or in a notebook for later review.
4. *Recite*. Taking time to recall, either by repeating aloud or even by sharing with a partner, helps solidify information that has been read. If the questions are unanswered or there is still a lack of clarity, rereading is essential before moving on.
5. *Review*. Review involves scanning over the notes and annotations made while reading or discussing the content. Or it may mean rereading the text. The critical consideration is to review the material to help maximize comprehension and memory.

The video entitled *SQ3R Reading method* (Jonson 2013) summarizes the key steps of the SQ3R method.

Reciprocal Teaching

Reciprocal teaching has been found by Hattie (2009) to be one of the most effective interventions in education, with an effect size of 0.74. Reciprocal teaching is an active reading strategy that was developed by Palincsar and Brown (1984) who also conducted trials to determine its effectiveness. They found that 70% of students improved their comprehension of what they were reading throughout five different passages, after using reciprocal teaching. In contrast, the control group did not improve their performance over the five passages. The experimental group functioned more independently and improved the quality of their summaries over time. Teachers also reported behavioral gains, with less time spent on behavior management in groups when using reciprocal teaching. Reciprocal teaching utilizes the skills of summarizing text, generating questions, clarifying, and predicting (Kelly, Moore & Tuck 1994). This strategy is used to help students with constructing meaning from the text as well as a means of monitoring their reading to ensure that they understand what they are reading. It is also a way of providing students who do not typically act as leaders in a small group to have a turn to do so since leadership opportunities alternate in the group.

A review of studies focused on reciprocal teaching practices found that when students worked in small groups and developed individual expertise in reading skills, they taught the skills to other group members and the overall understanding of the group members improved (Palincsar & Brown 1984). They also found that practicing using a reciprocal teaching activity provided students with opportunities to engage in actions that increased individual accountability within the group.

The reciprocal teaching process is frequently used in reading comprehension by small groups as they work together to discuss a book or topic. Individuals are assigned the roles of summarizer, questioner, clarifier, and predictor. Teachers prepare students for their roles through modeling and guided practice. In this way, students develop self-awareness about their role in the learning process and learn how to regulate their actions based on that awareness. Other related skills that are also taught and practiced include effective listening, note-taking, annotation, cross-referencing parts of the reading, and identifying relevant details.

Assigning roles and responsibilities helps set a purpose for the reading. Once clear about their roles, the students are given a reading passage. They individually read the same paragraphs or chapters, one at a time, pausing to fulfill their roles. The "*questioner*" asks questions about the content that seems to be challenging. The "*clarifier*" tries to answer any questions about parts of the text that were not clear or seem confusing. The "*predictor*" tries to develop ideas that they believe will be presented in the upcoming sections of the reading. The "*summarizer*" provides an overview of information from the content that has been read so far.

The teacher provides oversight and monitoring to ensure that students are fulfilling their roles and demonstrating understanding. A video from Mount Saint Mary College (2014), *Reciprocal Teaching*, demonstrates how a teacher works with students to prepare them for their reciprocal teaching roles in a secondary classroom.

Creating opportunities for students to learn to rely on each other as resources helps foster independence. The importance of empowering students to seek and use resources to gain independence is demonstrated in the video *Developing Independent Learners: Guiding Students to Be More Resourceful* (Edutopia. 2017).

KWL

The KWL method (Ogle 1986) uses a graphic organizer applicable to most content subjects. Upon introducing new topics, the KWL method stimulates and guides students to reflect on what they already *know*, *want to know*, and eventually *learned* about the topic after processing. It serves as a working document to organize information, as it provides students with a method to revisit and reflect on their thoughts. They record insights and details on their chart as they gather new information. The use of a KWL chart allows students to set individual goals by considering and registering unique things they find interesting. On the KWL chart, a student may respond in short responses or sentence responses depending on their goals and capabilities. For students challenged by writing, drawing a picture to depict their information is acceptable.

A video example from an elementary school in India entitled *K-W-L: Read with a purpose* (Teacher Pages 2015) provides an excellent example of a participative style of teaching children, using the KWL method, where every child in the class is attentive and benefits from learning from the strong communication skills of the teacher.

The KWL chart serves as a scaffolding technique to develop metacognitive awareness to support students in gathering, organizing, and processing information. KWL charts can be used to open and close any lesson and help students access background knowledge, formulate questions, and document information learned. It can also be used as a monitoring or tracking tool during reading, with students updating the answers to their questions in the "*learned*" section, and then formulating new questions in the "*want to know*" section as they read.

The chart is set up in three columns as follows:

Column 1: Things I Know (K): Give each student a KWL chart or have them draw one on a piece of paper. Initiate discussion with the students about what they already know about a new topic of study. Have them record the things they already know in the "K" column.

Column 2: Things I Want to Know (W): Discuss with students what they want to learn from the activity. They may process individually or with a partner if needed and record their responses.

Column 3: Things Learned (L): This occurs after the content is reviewed. Students note and discuss if they found the answer to any of their questions in the "W" column. Sharing and discussion of new information and related evidence are encouraged.

The video entitled *Teacher Toolkit: KWL High School* (Education Service Center Region13 2017a) demonstrates how students are encouraged to share their questions with a partner. The teacher also uses the responses from the KWL chart to determine what adjustments to comprehension are needed.

Anticipation Guide

Anticipation guides (Herber & Nelson-Herber 1993) are scaffolding tools that activate prior knowledge and provide information to help students anticipate the upcoming task/activity. It encourages students to process and record responses to statements ahead of and after discussion with peers.

An anticipation guide consists of a listing of several statements associated with the subject content. A guide is created by separating a page into three columns. Comments about the content are listed in the middle column. The left and right columns are titled "Before" and "After." Students read each statement before reviewing the content material, and then decide and record if they agree/disagree in the "Before" column. After conducting the activity, students revisit their original designation and update their opinion in the "After" column. Students share and discuss their views based on the evidence from the content.

Another video from Education Service Center Region13 (2017b), *Teacher Toolkit: Anticipation Guide Science*, demonstrates the use of an anticipation guide to prepare middle school students to start thinking about the content of an upcoming science project.

Think Aloud

As explained in Chap. 4, *Direct Instruction*, giving a student a model to follow is critical to understanding the expectations and sequence appropriate to complete a task. Think-aloud practices (Davey 1983) occur when teachers talk aloud as they demonstrate the process they are teaching. The use of effective "think aloud" relies heavily on teacher modeling followed by guided practice. The goal of "think aloud" is to actively demonstrate how skilled readers and problem solvers develop and organize their thoughts in order to process meaning (Farr & Conner 2015). The video *Go beyond a model; reveal a Think Aloud* (Smekens Education 2019) demonstrates the difference between telling students what to do and "concretely and precisely" walking them through the associated actions.

The sequence Davey (1983) recommends to teachers is as follows:

Select reading material: Select reading passages for students to practice. Prepare a reference list of questions for them to ponder during their independent reading.

Modeling: The teacher demonstrates by selecting a reading passage or a book and verbalizing about what predictions can be made based on the title or genre. After reading a few paragraphs or pages, the teacher pauses and makes further predictions based on the new information. They describe the visual images which the story content conjures up and pause at different parts of the text to highlight and make connections to other parts of the text. If the information is confusing or unexpected, the teacher verbalizes different methods for checking for understanding: for example, by stating, "I need to reread this section."

Student practice: Provide students with short passages to practice the "think aloud" process they have observed. As one student reads and practices thinking aloud, the other listens and similarly shares their thoughts.

Independent student practice using checklists: Students practice reading passages independently and periodically monitor their reading process by pausing to self-question, aided by a checklist to prompt their questioning.

Integrated use with other material: Guide and encourage students to apply the "think-aloud" skills to reading material from different content areas.

Additional "Think-Aloud" Tips

Teachers should provide cues by sharing thoughts about reading strategies they might use to aid comprehension. For example, "Maybe I will underline words that I think are important clues to what the text is about," or "I am going to jot a word or phrase down at the end of each paragraph to remind me what the paragraph was about."

To demonstrate actions to aid recall, the teacher may orally read and then make a comment such as "I will read the passage then stop at the end of the paragraph and tell a peer what I think the main idea is about."

Toward the end of a paragraph or section, encourage students to ask themselves questions. For example, "What was the main point, what kind of information did I learn?"

Conclusion

This chapter has outlined metacognitive strategies that are useful for teachers. However, throughout this book, several chapters have also provided examples of metacognitive strategies to improve student learning. These strategies included examples such as the use of rubrics, checklists, and feedback forms. Chapter three,

Formative Assessment, discussed the value of asking questions and observing work products to gain awareness of the depth of knowledge and understanding that is occurring. Chapter four, *Direct Instruction*, addressed the importance of scaffolding instruction using tools such as graphic organizers and visual charts to help students organize and label their thoughts and develop effective study skills. Chapter five, *Cooperative Learning*, identified the need for guidelines and reference charts against which cooperative groups could gauge the accuracy of their own work and performance. These are all metacognitive strategies which encourage students to reflect on their actions and learning processes and help guide their thinking around how to complete tasks accurately and efficiently.

References

Davey, B. (1983). Think aloud: Modeling the cognitive processes of reading comprehension. *The Journal of Reading, 27*, 44–47.

Education Endowment Foundation. (2021, October 28). *Teaching and learning toolkit*. EEF. https://educationendowmentfoundation.org.uk/education-evidence/teaching-learning-toolkit

Education Service Center Region13. (2017a, December 11). *Teacher toolkit: KWL (high school) [Video]*. YouTube. https://www.youtube.com/watch?v=NI1g-oDI_g0

Education Service Center Region13. (2017b, December 6). *Teacher toolkit: Anticipation guide science [Video]*. YouTube. https://www.youtube.com/watch?v=ED8JsrkKCmM

Edutopia. (2017, April 6). *Developing independent learners: Guiding students to be more resourceful [Video]*. YouTube. https://www.youtube.com/watch?v=IJD_IZOLfKU

Farr, R., & Connor, J. (2015). *Using think-Alouds to improve Reading comprehension*. Retrieved January 20, 2021 from https://www.readingrockets.org/article/using-think-alouds-improve-reading-comprehension.

Flavell, J. H. (1976). Metacognitive aspects of problem-solving. In L. B. Resnick (Ed.), *The nature of intelligence* (pp. 231–236). Erlbaum.

Hattie, J. A. C. (2009). *Visible learning: A synthesis of over 800 meta-analyses relating to achievement*. Routledge.

Herber, H. L., & Nelson-Herber, J. (1993). *Teaching in content areas with reading, writing, and reasoning*. Allyn and Bacon.

Jonson, J. (2013, June 12). *SQ3R reading method [Video]*. YouTube. https://www.youtube.com/watch?v=0dhcSP_Myjg

Kelly, M., Moore, D. W., & Tuck, B. F. (1994). Reciprocal teaching in a regular primary school classroom. *The Journal of Educational Research, 88*(1), 53–61.

Lucidchart. (2018, May 31). *How to make a concept map [Video]*. YouTube. https://www.youtube.com/watch?v=8XGQGhli0I0

McLeskey, J., Rosenberg, M. S., & Westling, D. L. (2013). *Inclusion: Effective practices for all students*. Pearson.

Memorize Academy. (2016, December 15). *How to study effectively for school or college [top 6 science-based study skills] [Video]*. YouTube. https://www.youtube.com/watch?v=CPxSzxylRCI

Mitchell, D., & Sutherland, D. (2020). *What really works in special and inclusive education: Using evidence-based teaching strategies* (3rd ed.). Routledge.

Mount Saint Mary College. (2014, May 7). *Reciprocal teaching [Video]*. YouTube. https://www.youtube.com/watch?v=TPVqXbbJZ54

Ogle, D. (1986). K-W-L: A teaching model that develops active reading of expository text. *The Reading Teacher, 39*, 564–570.

Palinscar, A., & Brown, A. (1984). Reciprocal teaching of comprehension-fostering and comprehension-monitoring activities. *Cognition and Instruction, 1*(2), 117–175.

Pintrich, P. (2002). The role of metacognitive knowledge in learning, teaching, and assessing. *Theory Into Practice, 41*(4), 219–225.

Putnam, A. L. (2015). Mnemonics in education: Current research and applications. *Translational Issues in Psychological Science, 1*(2), 130–139.

Robinson, F. P. (1946). *Effective study*. Harper & Brothers.

Scruggs, T., & Mastropieri, M. (2000). The effectiveness of mnemonic instruction for students with learning and behavior problems: An update and research synthesis. *Journal of Behavioral Education, 10*(2), 163–173.

Smekens Education. (2019, January 11). *Go beyond a model; reveal a Think Aloud [Video]*. YouTube. https://www.youtube.com/watch?v=UmhLgsBD1-I

Teacher Pages. (2015, April 17). *K-W-L: READ with a purpose! [Video]*. YouTube. https://www.youtube.com/watch?v=MCwHbPowvsE

Tiny Medicine. (2020, March 23). *Powerful mnemonic techniques (examples) [Video]*. YouTube. https://www.youtube.com/watch?v=axcPEKXhWJY

Chapter 8
Functional Behavior Assessment

Abstract This chapter provides information to guide evidence-based interventions to address behaviors that impede students' learning and interfere with classroom learning environments. Recommendations are made for ways to address the occurrence of disruptive behavior using a preventative approach. A tiered system of intervention is discussed, with emphasis first placed on school-wide and class-wide supports. Implementing functional behavior assessment (FBA) is considered in tier three when more targeted individual intervention becomes necessary. The chapter explains the FBA process and recommends procedures for conducting FBAs. Emphasis is placed on understanding the context surrounding the behavior to guide the selection of appropriate interventions. The importance of implementing plans using a team approach with thoughtful analysis of observed behaviors is highlighted. Additional strategies for managing behavior across grade levels are also discussed.

Rationale

Accomplishing a positive and productive classroom learning environment requires a structured classroom management system that clearly outlines and consistently enforces expectations, rules, routines, rewards, and consequences for behavior (Hattie & Zierer 2018; Wong et al. 2009). Well-implemented behavior management plans create classroom climates where students are highly engaged and participate with interest and intent. Effectively managed settings encourage students to cooperate with engaging activities to keep them focused on tasks that challenge and advance their learning (Marzano et al. 2003).

Evidence-based behavior management strategies, based on functional behavior assessment (FBA), have been demonstrated to positively impact student academic success, with an effect size of 0.52 (Hattie & Zierer 2018), indicating that FBA is an evidence-based teaching strategy. Classroom dynamics are fluid, and even in situations where behaviors are not currently problematic, small shifts in classroom dynamics can often alter this. The frequency, intensity, duration, or impact of a student's behavior can lead to significant disruptions that interfere with their own or

G. Hornby, D. Greaves, *Essential Evidence-Based Teaching Strategies*,
https://doi.org/10.1007/978-3-030-96229-6_8

others' academic and social success. Therefore, having procedures in place to address current and potential situations is critical. Emphasis is on using proactive approaches to prevent interfering behaviors from occurring. However, sometimes an individually designed behavior plan that outlines interventions to target specific student behaviors is warranted (Sugai et al. 2000).

National policies enacted in the USA under the Individuals with Disabilities Act (IDEA 2004) have recognized the impact of students' behavior on their learning and subsequent development of appropriate academic and social skills. These legal policies require schools to develop practices that identify the effects of misbehavior on student learning and then apply rigorously monitored interventions and adjust them according to ongoing data collection. It is critical to address behaviors proactively and with a well-informed and structured plan. This is critical for minimizing the negative impact that misbehavior can have on a student's learning.

In the UK, emphasis has been on adopting a whole-school approach to behavior management, setting teachers' strategies within a model that includes functional behavior assessment, and focusing on six key recommendations for improving behavior in schools. The six recommendations are: developing positive relationships by getting to know pupils and their context; facilitating pupil engagement by providing positive conditions for learning; using effective classroom management strategies; working collaboratively with parents using practical ideas such as daily greetings of children and holding breakfast clubs; targeting pupils with high behavior needs with specific strategies, such as behavior contracts; and working closely with colleagues to implement a whole-school approach to behavior management (Ellis & Tod 2018). School-wide behavior management practices must also consider the unique context of the school in the implementation plan. Successful plans pay attention to variables such as available resources, adequacy of training, extent to which interventions are data-driven and delivered with fidelity, and effectiveness of school leadership (Fox et al. 2021).

Many other countries have also focused on a whole-school approach to behavior management by adopting interventions based on tiered behavioral intervention systems and support. One such system is Positive Behavioral Interventions and Supports (PBIS), which is explained in the video entitled *What is PBIS? 5 minute description and 4 main components* (Mooiman 2020). Tiered systems of intervention typically have three tiers which represent a continuum of behavioral and academic supports. Tier 1 supports are focused on addressing the school-wide behavioral expectations. These interventions aim to prevent disruptive behaviors and may include giving students a break, allowing movement or other activities aimed at potential disruptions. Tier 2 supports are more targeted and address small groups of students with problem behaviors that do not respond to universal approaches. These may include inclusion in a social skill support group or academic tutoring support group. Conducting a functional behavior assessment is a more intensive tier 3 approach that addresses individual cases that remain unresponsive to tier 1 and tier 2 supports.

Theory

Skinner's (1953) seminal work linked behaviors with external conditioning, which impacts and changes behavior according to the individual's experiences. Subsequent research established significant correlations between behavior and external factors. More recent approaches focus on gathering and analyzing data to understand how and why individuals function in particular ways in various contexts and the use of data to determine appropriate ways to reshape conditions, reframe perceptions, and adapt responses to encourage appropriate and productive behaviors (Hanley 2012; Iwata & Dozier 2008). Understanding and intervening with students' behaviors are essential in school settings where students are required to comply with schools' expectations while also productively interacting with teachers and peers as they develop their skills (Stephenson & Hanley 2010).

When students demonstrate inappropriate behavior responses that are disruptive or potentially deleterious to the classroom's functioning, eliminating or at least reducing these behaviors is critical (Mueller & Nkosi 2007). Assessing the functions of behavior seeks to meaningfully understand individuals and the purpose of their actions by inquiring into and observing the behaviors under changing conditions. Functional behavior assessments (FBAs) seek to assess behaviors, identify triggers and consequences, and pinpoint effective interventions to encourage the appropriate action while diminishing the interfering behaviors (Hanley 2012). Initially, interventions provide direct external reinforcement to reward and support desired behaviors. Over time, students learn to generalize and maintain appropriate behaviors (Iwata & Dozier 2008; Ogier & Hornby 1996).

Preventative Measures

FBAs do not replace the need for well-planned and implemented measures to encourage an organized and smoothly functioning classroom. In many settings, there is a reliance on reactive management strategies, which are punitive, but frequently these methods are unsuccessful in bringing about lasting changes in behavior (Parsonson 2012). Developing, organizing, and maintaining a school and classroom climate conducive to teaching and learning provide several tiers of support foundational to an effective and well-managed classroom (Hattie & Timperley 2007). When developing management systems within the school setting, there are several aspects: the school-wide plan, the classroom plan, and the individual plan. The following guidelines, adapted from Parsonson (2012), Marzano et al. (2003), and Wong et al. (2009), are recommended to target plans at the school, classroom, and individual levels.

School-Wide Supports

At the school-wide level, measures must be put into place to support classroom management while setting the tone for the entire school. Teachers, parents, and students need to have shared awareness regarding acceptable behavior and clear expectations about who will address behavior situations as they occur. School districts typically have guidelines for acceptable codes of conduct. These expectations should be widely available, frequently reviewed, and consistently enforced.

School supports must also incorporate the following:

- Prepare teachers to address the myriad behaviors they will likely encounter by providing ongoing training.
- Provide time for teachers to collaborate and plan for both the academic and behavioral needs of their students.
- Appropriately place rules around the school buildings and in classrooms.
- Frequently review and reinforce rules.
- Focus on positive interventions rather than punitive ones.
- Implement consequences that advance from minimal to more restrictions.
- Deliver rewards consistently and across school settings. For example, schools will often have a tangible reinforcer, such as a ticket system, which students can earn in their classes and hallways as they navigate the building.
- Involve students in monitoring the rewards they earn.

Classroom Supports

As proactive management plans are developed, they should be monitored and adjusted as appropriate to the setting. Teachers must be aware and clear about potential areas which need preparation and planning (Wong et al. 2009). This includes having protocols and plans to address behaviors related to how students gather materials, clean up, take tests, work cooperatively, take turns, use, and access technology. As teachers plan lessons, they must consider how students act and respond during the activities. Though it may not be possible to prepare for every eventuality, school staff can anticipate many situations. Several key recommendations from Parsonson (2012) are discussed below.

Establishing Clear Rules

Teachers should work together with students to set specific classroom rules appropriate to the class's nuances. These rules should be shared to clarify understanding. Some students may need a pictorial representation to understand what an appropriate action looks like: for example, a visual of a raised hand to indicate how to get the teacher's attention. Additionally, students should be allowed to practice the appropriate steps required to follow the rules.

A video from San Bernardino City Schools (2019), entitled *Teaching procedures, routines and rules during the first week of school in fourth grade*, demonstrates how a teacher explicitly prepares her students for daily routines and procedures. The teacher engages students by giving examples and practicing day-to-day rituals and rules related to movement and transitions to ensure that they are aware and ready to function in an organized and respectful manner. What is apparent from the depiction is that taking time to put measures in place is highly valued. The need for explicit instruction around rules and routines is essential, and teachers must prepare and scaffold behavior learning just as they would for academic work.

Managing Noise, Movement, and Transitions

It is important to establish how students should enter and exit the classroom. For example, if there are students in the school with wheelchairs, there must be clarity about how those students will navigate in the setting. There should be directives about how paperwork will be distributed and collected and what activities allow increased volume and chatter among students.

Establishing Classroom Incentives

There must be clarity about what rewards are allowed and whether they will be delivered individually or to the group. Teachers and students should have a shared understanding of the frequency and timing for administering rewards.

Enhancing Engagement

Involving students in the daily routines of the class helps to foster engagement. Assigning leadership roles is a method to include students in these routines. When students take turns satisfying different leadership roles, the responsibilities and expectations for fulfilling those roles must be explicit. For example, functions can include line leader, material organizer, paperwork collector or distributor, rules reviewer, or classroom monitor. Engagement is also enhanced when instruction and student work are varied to allow different forms of instruction and ways for students to demonstrate their learning.

Building Relationships and Peer Support

Spending time conferring with students and having meaningful exchanges helps build relationships. Students should also have opportunities to engage respectfully with each other. Rules about appropriately addressing each other and addressing the teacher during conversations must be established and enforced. Trust also helps students engage with their peers, making them feel welcome and part of a community. When students feel that their contributions are valued, they are more open to engagement and taking a chance even if they are unsure or uncertain (Darling-Hammond & Cook-Harvey 2018). It is helpful to assign activities for students to work with partners on assignments and be explicit and clear about good peer relations: for example, checking to ensure that a peer has the correct homework assignment or reviewing a work completion checklist with a peer.

For some students, school is a haven from which they can escape unpleasant circumstances they may encounter elsewhere (Scherer 1997). Taking time to foster relationships by showing an interest in students is essential. The video *Making connections with greetings at the door* (Edutopia 2019a) demonstrates how connections are made as teachers at an elementary school meet their students at the door to acknowledge them and engage in brief, positive verbal exchanges to start the day. Several teachers explain why they believe these greetings are so important. One teacher in the video noted that it helps to have a "pulse check" to determine students' emotions as they start their day. Yet another video example, *The power of relationships in schools* (Edutopia 2019b), demonstrates and reinforces the importance of teacher-student relationships, which is addressed in greater detail in Chapter two.

Individual Supports

Though staff may consistently implement school-wide and class-wide plans, there are still situations where behavior may escalate to extremely inappropriate and disruptive levels. In these instances, a functional behavior assessment (FBA) is warranted. When behavior is unique to one student, considering and investigating causes are necessary. Individual support may include developing an individual behavior contract with specific reinforcement systems. Teachers or counselors should participate in collaborative conferences with individual students. These conferences seek to inquire into the observed behaviors and give students a chance to share their perspectives and reflect on their behaviors. It also helps give teachers insight into what adjustments the student may need.

Conducting a Functional Behavior Assessment (FBA)

FBAs may not be needed for behaviors that are not intense or frequent or do not occur for a lengthy duration. However, even in cases where behaviors are troublesome but have not yet escalated in a significant way, incorporating FBA steps helps teachers reflect on and monitor their practices to understand how current classroom structures and interactions encourage or hinder appropriate behavioral responses. A helpful framework from Ditrano (2010) incorporates functional, descriptive, and indirect measures to outline a process for conducting FBAs. The first step is identifying and defining the problem behavior and gathering data to understand the child's behavior. Next, a purposeful analysis of all relevant information is used to form a hypothesis about the problem behavior, the purpose it seems to serve, and the conditions which seem to reinforce it. A plan is developed, implemented, monitored, and adjusted according to ongoing data collection. Teachers, students, parents, and other relevant staff are critical to the effective collection of data and the success of FBAs.

Involving Parents, Teachers, Students, and Relevant Staff

There are child protection laws in many countries to ensure that students' confidentiality and due process rights are protected. Therefore, parental consent or awareness is typically required to initiate the FBA process. Teacher participation on behavior management teams is critical. They provide valuable anecdotal and more structured formal insights through interviews and behavioral questionnaires. Students encounter multiple teachers throughout their day. Therefore, gathering data from different teachers often warrants their involvement. Teachers can provide data about what they have observed, interventions tried, and which management strategies had minimal or no impact on the behaviors of concern. Teachers also play a pivotal role in implementing the behavior plan as they are typically required to manage the plans and collect ongoing data about the behaviors. Often, school counselors, psychologists, or school principals are involved. Students also have a role to play in providing insight into their behaviors and should be included at some level in the process.

Functional Analysis

FBAs include a series of actions taken to identify the behavior, define the problem, and investigate, implement, and monitor solutions. According to Hanley (2012), there are three components to FBAs: functional analysis, descriptive assessment, and indirect assessment. The functional analysis involves observing the behavior of concern while the environmental conditions are manipulated to determine how the changing conditions affect the behavior. As researchers point out, this can be a lengthy and detailed process, and those involved should be well trained in the nuances of the process (Iwata et al. 2008; Mueller & Nkosi 2007). In schools across America, school psychologists or trained behavior interventionists typically oversee and coordinate the FBA process.

Functional analysis is explained and clarified in a video from Fuqua (2015) entitled *Functional analysis of problem behavior*. It explains the scientific basis and data-gathering procedures appropriate for collecting data and analyzing behaviors as they occur. A critical insight from the video is that identifying the problem behavior and replacing it with appropriate behaviors require manipulation of reinforcement conditions to determine the most effective intervention.

Descriptive Assessment

Descriptive assessments help identify and define the problem. This stage of the process seeks to attain information about what behaviors the student is engaging in and how these interfere with or impede the student and others around them. At the level of the classroom, this would likely be an observable action. Observers should note the timing, location, and events before, during, and after the occurrence. Also important is information about who was present and what was expected of the student. Establishing clarity about the problem helps the plan to have a specific focus and be appropriate for addressing the particular behavior(s). Tools to support descriptive assessments are the following:

Observations: Anecdotal notes are collected at different times of the day and during different types of activities. Teachers may jot down free-flowing notes to describe behaviors, settings, and interactions. It is helpful to have others conduct similar observations to gather multiple perspectives.

ABC information: Observations are recorded on a blank template referred to as an ABC chart. The antecedents (A) provide insight into what occurs before the behavior(s). The observable behaviors (B) are the behaviors of concern that occur during the observation time. The consequences (C) describe what happens after the behavior occurs and provide insight into the extent to which the actions following the behavior(s) cause it to escalate, diminish, or remain unchanged.

In the video entitled *Functional Behavior Analysis: Conducting an ABC Analysis* (The IRIS Center 2018a), the step-by-step collection and use of ABC observation data are shared and demonstrated for its value in understanding and responding to students' lack of compliance and refusal to do their work. In the example, the teacher first explains the task to the class. Under antecedents, the teacher makes notes about their actions prior to the onset of the student's behavior. The time of the event is also noted. The consequences are documented as the action the teacher takes immediately following the noncompliant behavior. This process of observing and recording evolving ABC data continues for a designated time. Information is later analyzed to better understand the patterns of behavior and how the antecedents and consequences may impact the behavior.

Indirect Assessment

Indirect assessments utilize responses to interviews and questionnaires to identify the functions of behaviors. This method also provides insight into student likes, dislikes, and rewards that they may find appealing and how they respond in different settings. This information is sought from those who frequently interact with the student of concern through the following means:

Checklists/questionnaires/interviews: When analyzed, interviews and questionnaires can provide understanding about how students respond to various people and settings. For example, insights are gained about whether the student behaves more appropriately with specific individuals than others, or does involvement in certain activities increase or reduce episodes of inappropriate behavior? The information collected encourages more informed decision-making about motives for the behavior. Whether attention-seeking or being motivated by fear or avoidance, control, or retaliation, knowledge about potential reasons helps determine appropriate ways to intervene with the student (Iwata & Dozier 2008).

Review of student records: Records collected as part of the ongoing school-wide data collection process can provide useful information about the student. Grade books, attendance reports, home-to-school communication logs, work samples, progress reports, and individual education plans (IEPs) are all sources that provide insights or may reveal patterns of concern. For example, frequent late arrival or frequent absence due to illness may cause missed instruction. Similarly, suppose the student tends to misbehave in one class more than in another. In that case, consideration may be given to the varying degrees of difficulty experienced or the expectations and requirements for each class.

Summarizing and analyzing the information: Summarizing requires organizing the information and taking a reflective approach to looking at what has occurred. Analyzing helps develop an understanding of how the student benefits by engaging in the behavior(s) of concern. This involves looking at the context of the behaviors, looking for patterns, and considering if relationships between different factors are contributing to the interfering behavior. Meeting as a team to review and discuss the findings assures multiple perspectives and safeguards against potential bias as plans are formulated.

Whatever the student's motivation(s), it is critical that teachers and school staff approach and craft their responses to the situations against the background of a well-formulated hypothesis that considers the antecedents, behaviors, consequences, frequency, intensity, and duration. They also need to consider all the daily demands on and suitability of tasks for the student. Summarizing and analyzing all the data help teachers and school-based staff reflect on the students and their behavior and formulate hypotheses about what is causing the behavior and what responses are likely to be the most effective toward bringing about change.

Developing Behavior Intervention Plans (BIP)

Once behavior assessments are conducted and discussed, teams can identify appropriate interventions. These interventions and their application become part of a behavior intervention plan (BIP). The purpose of a BIP is to develop replacement behaviors that allow students to have a more productive learning experience that increases their potential for reaching their learning targets (Farmer & Floyd 2016; Iwata et al. 2008). Although behavior plans focus on a student's behaviors, they also require simultaneously considering and monitoring the appropriateness of the adult actions and the school's practices in response to these behaviors.

Implementing the BIP

When implementing a BIP, there are several keys to its success:

- Behavior interventions should be applied with consistency across all identified settings.
- Reinforcement for the replacement behavior must be timely and consistently delivered.
- The focus of actions should be maintained on the identified target behavior and its replacement behavior.
- Using one plan to address multiple behaviors should normally be avoided.
- Focus must be maintained on the interventions listed in the plan.
- If any changes to the plan are needed, those involved with the student should be informed and updated and participate in the changes, based on the data collected across settings.
- Adults involved in implementing the plan must be informed and shown how to administer parts of the plan. For example, if a checklist is to accompany the child from one setting to another, all teachers must be vigilant to insert their input onto the checklist before the child leaves their class.
- Data must be collected exactly as directed by the plan.

Monitoring and Modifying the BIP

Updated information about behavior identifies what has changed and the extent to which interventions are practical or effective. The plan should be adjusted and modified according to the observed changes in circumstances and behavior. All participants, including students, parents, and involved school staff, should be informed of any updates when monitoring the plan. Frequent team meetings should occur to check on the student's progress and the internal consistency of the plan. Data (observations, checklists, behavior monitoring forms) should be collected and reviewed regularly.

The importance of the steps noted above is summarized in the video from The IRIS Center 2018b), entitled *A Summary of Functional Behavioral Analysis (FBA)*.

Strategies for Preschool and Elementary Students

Visual Schedules

The goal of a visual schedule is for the student to become independent with using the schedule to start, stop, and transition to the activities that form their daily routine (Hume 2009). For children with significant or severe behavior challenges related to sudden changes in routine, or difficulty starting and stopping a routine, a visual schedule using pictures or actual props as cues, words, or a combination of these helps them to organize and process their daily routines and specific tasks within the day (e.g., going to the bathroom, cleaning up). Visual schedules require preparation and careful explicit instruction and demonstration until the student becomes independent with each of the steps, as follows:

- Visual or tangible cues are prepared to depict key activities and tasks.
- Cues are laid out in sequence to depict the activity or the student's transition.
- The sequenced cues may be designed for removal by the student to signify that they have completed a task or are ready to start the next one.
- Students are encouraged to practice using their schedules to develop independence.

Check-in and Checkout

At the start of the class session, the teacher "*checks in*" with the student to review behavioral goals and expectations. The teacher monitors and evaluates the student's behavior and gives the student a score on a Behavior Report Card. A "checkout" is conducted after a predetermined time (end of the day or end of a class session). The teacher meets with the student, and the student evaluates the extent to which they believe they reached their goals. The teacher then shares the scores based on their monitoring and discusses them with the student. If the student has earned a reward or incentive, the teacher rewards them and praises them for their work. If the student fails to earn the reward, the teacher provides corrective feedback, encouragement, and guidance about improving during the next "check-in."

The video entitled *Check-In/Check-Out: Providing a daily support system for students* (Edutopia 2018) explains the use of the check-in/checkout system with students and teachers as they meet to conduct reviews and reiterate expectations with students. Several students also share their opinions about how frequent meetings with an adult help remind them of their expectations and stay on track with their routines.

Strategies for Middle and High School Students

The Student-Teacher Game

The student-teacher game is appropriate for middle and high school students. It is designed around the philosophy of changing behavior by focusing on rewarding positive outcomes and reteaching when outcomes are adverse (Barrish et al. 1969; Embry 2002). It does not focus on punitive actions. It is conducted with the entire class but can occur with the teacher breaking the larger class into smaller groups. The idea is for the teacher to notice the students when they appropriately follow a rule surrounding a particular routine or activity and reward them when they behave appropriately.

During the game, the following sequence is applied:

- Teachers and students agree to the behavior which needs improvement, and which will be monitored: for example, returning from lunch break and settling into the next class routine quickly and organized.
- A time frame for monitoring and earning points is determined. For the example given above, this may be identified as the 3–4-min window during which students reenter the classroom after their lunch break.
- Specific behaviors which will earn points are clarified (e.g., entering the room quietly, sitting at assigned seats, and starting the activity on the board).
- The method of allocating points is clarified. For example, one point is earned for each of the appropriate behaviors demonstrated. Students should be included in self-monitoring by also recording and charting their earned points.
- Students receive earned points or rewards at the end of the designated time.
- When students are not accomplishing a positive outcome, the teachers or other group members continue to work directly with them to revisit, reteach, and practice the appropriate behaviors.

Behavior Contracts

A common type of behavior contract functions on the premise that behaviors can be shaped by receipt of a token reward system which individuals earn when they engage in specific behaviors. This approach has been found to effectively alter behavior (Kazdin & Bootzin 1972).

Establishing a behavior contract requires several steps:

- Identify and specify the behavior to be improved.
- Develop the rewards that can be earned. Select several inexpensive rewards such as tickets to trade for a prize, such as computer time, time to draw or color in a personal sketch pad, or lunch with a friend.

- Explain and clarify what student actions will earn a reward. Include the expected behavior, the time frame, and the consequences. For example, "When the verbal direction is given to clean up, Debbie will pick up her activity materials and return them to their storage areas in 2-3 minutes."
- Take time to meet with students to explain and demonstrate how the contract works. Keep it simple and use visual support to explain the contract to younger students.
- For older students, parents and teachers can sign the contract as a symbol of its importance and shared agreement.
- Implement and meet in established time frames to review progress with the student and monitor the contract for progress.

The video entitled *How To Use A Behavior Contract in 15-Minutes.wmv* (Woods 2010) provides additional insights into how to create a behavior contract. These can be applied to any student who needs a more individual approach.

Suggestions to support the effective use of behavior contracts include the following:

- Keep a behavior checklist or behavior chart to notate or chart progress that is shared with the student.
- Frequently refer to the contract with the student.
- Administer rewards as agreed.
- Be consistent with providing the reward.
- Change rewards if they are not motivating.
- Check to be sure that the expected behavior is something the student can actually do. For example, if the student has a diagnosis of attention deficit disorder, a goal of staying in an assigned seat to complete a written task for 30 minutes may be too lofty.

Conclusion

Conducting a functional behavior assessment (FBA) provides a blueprint to guide a plan of action for teachers. Contracts help to guide students toward appropriate behaviors that do not interfere with their learning and others' learning. These plans may require frequent monitoring and revision as learning environments change. Frequently, the behaviors and emotions which students manifest may appear to go beyond the realm of what a teacher believes they can impact. However, it is critical to have procedures in place to allow all students to benefit from instruction and social learning experiences in the classroom. The FBA process and the behavior plans that emerge from that process provide such a protocol. When developed and implemented as outlined in this chapter, these protocols address interfering behaviors in a way that is tailored to students' needs.

References

Barrish, H. H., Saunders, M., & Wolf, M. M. (1969). Good behavior game: Effects of individual contingencies for group consequences on disruptive behavior in a classroom. *Journal of Applied Behavior Analysis, 2*(2), 119–124.

Darling-Hammond, L., & Cook-Harvey, C. M. (2018). *Educating the whole child: Improving school climate to support student success (research brief)*. Learning Policy Institute.

Ditrano, C. (2010). *Functional behavior assessment and behavior intervention plans*. Dude.

Edutopia. (2018, February 5). *Check-in/check-out: providing a daily support system for students [Video]*. YouTube. https://www.youtube.com/watch?v=MyPUY38blZQ

Edutopia. (2019a, January 14). *Making connections with greetings at the door [Video]*. YouTube. https://www.youtube.com/watch?v=GVAKBnXIGxA&feature=youtu.be

Edutopia. (2019b, January 14). *The power of relationships in schools [Video]*. YouTube. https://www.youtube.com/watch?v=kzvm1m8zq5g

Ellis, S., & Tod, J. (2018). *Behavior for learning: Promoting positive relationships in the classroom*. Routledge.

Embry, D. D. (2002). The good behavior game: A best practice candidate as a universal behavioral vaccine. *Clinical Child and Family Psychology Review, 5*(4), 273–297.

Farmer, R., & Floyd, R. (2016). An evidence-driven, solution-focused approach to functional behavior assessment report writing: FBA report writing. *Psychology in the Schools, 53*(10), 1018–1031.

Fox, R., Leif, E., Moore, D., Furlonger, B., Anderson, A., & Sharma, U. (2021). A systematic review of the facilitators and barriers to the sustained implementation of school-wide positive behavioral interventions and supports. *Education and Treatment of Children*. https://doi.org/10.1007/s43494-021-00056-0

Fuqua, W. (2015, January 30). *Functional analysis of problem behavior [Video]*. YouTube. https://www.youtube.com/watch?v=2RFq13r3khY

Hanley, G. P. (2012). Functional assessment of problem behavior: Dispelling myths, overcoming implementation obstacles, and developing new lore. *Behavior Analysis in Practice, 5*(1), 54–72.

Hattie, J., & Timperley, H. (2007). The power of feedback. *Review of Educational Research, 77*(1), 81–112.

Hattie, J., & Zierer, K. (2018). *10 mindframes for visible learning*. Routledge.

Hume, K. (2009). Steps for implementation: Visual schedules. In *The National Professional Development Center on autism Spectrum disorders, frank porter Graham child development institute*. University of North Carolina.

IDEA. (2004). Individuals with Disabilities Education Act, 20 U.S.C. § 1400.

Iwata, B., & Dozier, C. L. (2008). Clinical application of functional analysis methodology. *Behavior Analysis in Practice, 1*(1), 3–9.

Kazdin, A. E., & Bootzin, R. R. (1972). The token economy: An evaluative review. *Journal of Applied Behavior Analysis, 5*(3), 343–372.

Marzano, R. J., Marzano, J. S., & Pickering, D. (2003). *Classroom management that works: Research-based strategies for every teacher*. Association for Supervision and Curriculum Development.

Mooiman, L. (2020, August 26). *What is PBIS? 5 minute description and 4 main components [Video]*. YouTube. https://www.youtube.com/watch?v=x_KDFb_SSc0

Mueller, M., & Nkosi, A. (2007). State of the science in the assessment and management of severe behavior problems in school settings: Behavior analytic consultation to schools. *International Journal of Behavioral Consultation and Therapy, 3*(2), 176–202.

Ogier, R., & Hornby, G. (1996). Effects of differential reinforcement on the behavior and self-esteem of children with emotional and behavioral disorders. *Journal of Behavioral Education, 6*(4), 501–510.

Parsonson, B. (2012). Evidence-based classroom behavior management strategies. *Kairaranga, 13*, 16–23.

San Bernardino City Schools. (2019, August 30). *Teaching procedures, routines, and rules during the first week of school in fourth grade [Video]*. YouTube. https://www.youtube.com/watch?v=vaedonG8-_Q

Scherer, M. (1997). Schools as safe havens. *Educational Leadership, 55*(2), 5.

Skinner, B. F. (1953). *Science and human behavior*. Macmillan.

Stephenson, K. M., & Hanley, G. (2010). Preschoolers' compliance with simple instructions: A descriptive and experimental evaluation. *Journal of Applied Behavior Analysis, 43*(2), 229–247.

Sugai, G., Lewis-Palmer, T., & Hagan-Burke, E. (2000). Overview of the functional behavioral assessment process. *Exceptionality, 8*(3), 149–160.

The IRIS Center video collection. (2018a, February 1). *Functional behavioral assessment: Conducting an ABC analysis [Video]*. YouTube. https://www.youtube.com/watch?v=Sxf9GPH5A-8

The IRIS Center video collection. (2018b, February 1). *A summary of functional behavioral analysis (FBA) [Video]*. YouTube. https://www.youtube.com/watch?v=NFHck-X43y4

Wong, H. K., Wong, R. T., & Seroyer, C. (2009). *The first days of school: How to be an effective teacher*. Harry K. Wong.

Woods, M. (2010, September 16). *How to use a behavior contract in 15-minutes.wmv [Video]*. YouTube. https://www.youtube.com/watch?v=BnUvQTvmtj0

Chapter 9
Parental Engagement

Abstract This chapter examines the rationale for the importance of parental engagement in education and the research evidence base supporting its effectiveness in improving children's outcomes. A theoretical model for parental engagement that helps teachers focus on parents' needs and their potential contributions is presented. Essential practical strategies for implementing this model and developing effective working relationships with parents are outlined. Examples of parental engagement in the early years, elementary, middle school, and high school levels are provided, supplemented by video clips.

Rationale

Parental engagement and parental involvement are terms used to refer to the involvement of parents with their children's education both at school and at home and have been found to provide effective strategies for improving educational achievement (Goodall 2013; Jeynes 2018; Wilder 2014). The UK *Teaching and Learning Toolkit* (Education Endowment Foundation 2021) reports that it has a moderate impact, based on moderate evidence. Hattie (2009) found the effect size for parental involvement to be 0.51 for schools overall, whereas Jeynes (2005, 2007) reported it to be between 0.70 and 0.74 for urban primary schools and between 0.38 and 0.53 for urban secondary schools. These findings confirm that parental engagement/involvement is an evidence-based practice based on extensive research conducted from early childhood through to high school levels.

So it is clear that parent engagement is an important evidence-based practice that all teachers need to be effective in facilitating. This is illustrated by Karen Mapp in the brief video entitled *Part—"On the Same Page—Families and Schools as Partners"*. In this video from Every Person Influences Children NYC (2010) it is suggested that schools can be viewed as on a continuum with regard to the quality of parent and family engagement, with four types of schools on this continuum.

The four types of schools are:

1. *A Fortress School*: Not a friendly place for families; some teachers say, "our parents don't care about their kid's education."
2. *A Come If We Call School*: We will call you when we want you to come to school, you do not call us.
3. *An Open-Door School*: Trying to engage parents, have an action team for families, but school centric, not parent centric.
4. *A Partnership School*: Parents involved in decision-making, teachers going into the community, doing home visits, doing parent programs at a community center, everybody working together to support children's learning.

It is clear from the above that effective parent and family engagement requires a partnership between teachers and families that involves sharing expertise to provide the optimum education for children (Epstein 2000; Grant & Ray 2010, Henderson & Mapp 2002). When the principles of such partnerships are developed, schools can establish effective collaborative working relationships between teachers, parents, and other family members. The brief video from Moriah College (2018) entitled According to Turnbull et al. (2011), there are seven principles of effective partnerships between teachers and parents: trust, respect, competence, communication, commitment, equality, and advocacy. However, several factors can act as barriers to meaningful parent engagement.

Barriers to Effective Parent Involvement

The issue of parental involvement in education is notable for the rhetoric supporting it and considerable variation in the reality of its practice. An explanation for the gap between rhetoric and reality regarding such involvement is that several factors are acting as barriers to effective parental involvement (Hornby 2011). Being aware of the various types of barriers enables teachers to gain greater insight into the factors that act as barriers and the factors that can facilitate effective parental engagement. This allows teachers to develop more effective practices regarding parental involvement in education.

There are four types of barriers to establishing effective parental engagement in education (Hornby & Lafaele 2011). First, there are individual parent and family factors that act as barriers. These focus on parents' beliefs about parental involvement; parents' current life contexts; parents' perceptions of invitations for involvement; and class, ethnicity, and gender. Second, various child factors can act as barriers, including the child's age; any learning difficulties or disabilities; the presence of gifts and talents; and behavioral problems. Third, parent-teacher factors can act as barriers, including focusing on differing agendas and the different attitudes and languages used by each person. Fourth, societal factors can be barriers to parental engagement, including historical and demographic issues, political issues, and economic issues. Teachers seeking to develop partnerships with parents and implement effective parental engagement need to address all four types of barriers. For such partnerships to be realized, these barriers need to be viewed as the context within which a model for parental engagement is developed.

Theoretical Approach to Facilitating Effective Parent Engagement

A theoretical model for parental engagement is necessary to provide teachers with a framework for working with parents. The model developed by Hornby (2000) helps teachers focus on parents' needs being met and their potential contributions being utilized. This makes teachers aware of addressing parents' needs and acknowledging the various ways that parents can contribute to their children's education.

The theoretical model for parental engagement was developed by combining and adapting existing models (e.g., Epstein 2000, 2018) and gaining feedback from numerous groups of parents, teachers, and other professionals working in schools. The model for parental engagement has been used by the author for the past 30 years in teacher education and professional development courses. The model consists of two aspects, one focusing on parents' needs, and the other on parents' strengths or potential contributions. Each of the model components is outlined below, and more details are available in Hornby (2000, 2011).

Parental Needs

Channels of Communication

Parents need to have effective channels of communication with their children's teachers. They need information about the organization and requirements of the school as it affects their child. They need to know when their children are having difficulties and what the school will do to address these. Also, parents need information about their rights and responsibilities. Schools can provide this information through handbooks or newsletters written especially for parents. Parents need to feel that they can contact the school at any time when they have a concern about their child. Some parents prefer to communicate by telephone, and others would rather go in to see the teacher face-to-face, while still others find that contact through email or text messages or written notes suits them best.

Liaison with School Staff

Parents want to know how their children are getting on at school. They want to find out what their children have achieved and whether they are having any difficulties. They regard teachers as the main source of information on their children's performance at school and therefore need to have a working partnership with them. Teachers can facilitate this by keeping in regular contact with parents through telephone calls, home visits, home-school notebooks, weekly report cards, and meeting with parents at school. These strategies are discussed later in the chapter.

Parent Education

Many parents are interested in receiving guidance from teachers to promote their children's progress or manage their behavior. Parent education is an important service that schools can provide. This is illustrated by the brief video from Northern California Public Media (2016) entitled *The Importance of Parental Involvement*.

Many parents are interested in participating in parent education programs at their child's schools. An effective format for parent education programs combines guidance about promoting children's development with opportunities for parents to discuss their concerns. Parent education programs that involve a group of parents, and employ a workshop format, easily lend themselves to providing a combination of educational input and sharing of concerns. This type of format enables parents to learn new skills and gain confidence through talking to other parents and teachers (Hornby & Murray 1983).

Parent Support

Some parents, at some times, need supportive counseling. Whereas most parents are reluctant to seek the help of professional counselors, they will approach their children's teachers in search of guidance or counseling for the problems that concern them. Therefore, teachers need to be good listeners to help parents solve everyday problems and know when to refer parents to professional counselors when issues raised are beyond their level of competence (Hornby, Hall & Hall 2003).

Parental Contributions

Policy Formation

Some parents can contribute their expertise through membership in parent or professional organizations. This includes being a school governor or a member of the parent-teacher association, or involvement in parent support or advocacy groups.

Others can provide in-service training for professionals by speaking at conferences or workshops or writing about their experiences. Teachers should continually be on the lookout for parents who can contribute in this way so that their abilities are used to the fullest. Parents should especially be involved in the development of school policy for parental engagement. The Australian Institute for Teaching and School Leadership (2016) has an example of this in the video entitled *Leading parental engagement initiatives*, which shows how teachers at a school in Australia involved parents in developing a whole-school policy for parent engagement.

Acting as a Resource

Many parents have the time and ability to act as voluntary teacher aides, either assisting in the classroom, or in the preparation of materials, or in fundraising. Others may have special skills that they can contribute, such as helping prepare newsletters, craft activities, or curriculum areas in which they have a unique talent. Some parents may have the time, skills, and knowledge to support other parents either informally or perhaps through participation in self-help or support groups. They may acquire knowledge that is helpful to their understanding of their children. In addition, they are often observed to gain confidence by helping at school and becoming motivated to further their education.

Collaborating with Teachers

Most parents are able to collaborate with teachers by reinforcing classroom programs such as home-school reading programs. However, teachers have to accept that some parents at some points in time are simply not able to collaborate in this way. Teachers must respect parents' rights to make this decision in consideration of the broader needs of their families. So, while involvement in home-school programs, or other requests for parents to carry out work with their children at home, should always be offered to all parents, including those who have not collaborated in the past, it should be expected that a small proportion of parents will not participate. Therefore, teachers need the skills to collaborate with parents in a flexible partnership in which parents' choices are respected.

Sharing Information on Children

Parents can contribute valuable information about their children because they have known them throughout their lives and have been the ones who have participated in all previous contacts with professionals to plan for meeting their children's needs. For example, information concerning children's likes and dislikes, strengths, and weaknesses, along with any relevant medical details, can be gathered by teachers at parent-teacher meetings. Making full use of parents' knowledge of their children makes parents feel that they have been listened to and an active interest has been taken in their children.

Strategies and Interventions for Effective Parental Engagement

In order to implement this model, teachers need to develop effective practical strategies for working with parents. These include strategies for encouraging parents to go into schools, conducting effective parent-teacher meetings, and communicating with parents in written forms through newsletters, notes sent home, home-school diaries, and progress reports. It also includes the use of telephone contacts, text messages, email, and, when necessary, making home visits. Brief guidelines for psychologists, counselors, and teachers about implementing these various forms of parental involvement strategies in schools are presented below, with more details provided in Hornby (2000, 2011).

Strategies for Encouraging Parents into School

Informal events provide a means whereby parents and school staff can meet each other as people with a mutual interest in building relationships on behalf of children, thereby helping to break down the barriers that often exist between school and home. There are several types of informal activities that encourage parents into schools: school productions in which they see their children perform in some way or the other; open days, gala days, or school fairs that provide opportunities for teachers and parents to meet informally; and various school outings into the local community that include teachers, parents, and other family members. The brief video from Moriah College (2018) entitled *Primary School Open Day 2018* shows photos from an open day at an Australian primary school. Parents were shown examples of what the school offered, and they had opportunities to meet informally with teachers and other parents.

Parent-Teacher Meetings

A key strategy that all schools use is that of parent-teacher interviews or meetings. These meetings are an established method of involving parents, and research has shown that they impact both parent-teacher relationships and student progress (Hornby 2011). It is important to both participants that they are organized to ensure effective communication. To achieve this, schools should focus on plans for tasks to occur before and after meetings and on appropriate protocols for conducting meetings.

A particularly effective approach to parent-teacher meetings is known as "student-led parent-teacher meetings" (Little & Allan 1989; Kinney 2005). In this approach, children introduce their parents to their teacher, who then shows selected samples of their work to parents. Teachers then discuss children's achievements, strengths, and areas for development. Parents, teachers, and children then work together to set goals for the student. An example of a student-led parent-teacher meeting is demonstrated in the video *Student Led Parent Teacher Conference—Middle School* (Raise the Bar Parents 2014) with a middle school student, her father, and her class teacher. A second example is from a rural middle-high school in the USA with double the average proportion of students from low SES backgrounds. The video from Julie Mazzolli Productions (2014) is entitled *In Charge: Student-led Conferences.* Information reported in the video states that when the school changed from traditional parent-teacher meetings to student-led conferences, the attendance of parents increased from 10% to 90%.

Written Communication

Schools can use various forms of written communication to inform and communicate with parents. The most commonly used are school or class newsletters, handbooks for parents, and children's progress reports. Letters, notes sent home, and home-school diaries are also widely used. However, there are two major difficulties with this form of communication. First, if some of the pupils' parents do not have English as their first language, then ideally, every written communication with parents needs to be translated into the appropriate language. Second, it is important to remember that some parents have reading difficulties themselves. This video clip, entitled *Everybody Writes: Creating a school newsletter* (Book Trust 2011), shows how the children at a British primary school were involved in producing class newsletters.

Telephone Contacts

Many parents are comfortable communicating with teachers through the telephone, and many parents prefer to maintain contact with teachers in this way. Many parents appreciate the opportunity of being able to phone teachers directly. So, it is usually best to get the school secretary to take messages and tell parents that the teacher will phone back as soon as possible. Teachers can check whether parents are at home during the day or are comfortable being called at work, in which case at least some of the calls can be made from school during the day.

Technological Options for Communication

Communication options such as email, WhatsApp, and text messaging have great potential for increasing effective parental involvement. Text messaging provides a means of sharing information and contacting parents urgently, as in the case of sickness or an injury to their child. School websites can provide information about contacting staff and present details of current and forthcoming activities and home activities for parents to engage with children. School and class newsletters sent out by email can be used to highlight class activities, enabling parents to share in their children's experiences and support their children's learning at home.

Home Visits

Some parents, especially those with special needs children, appreciate it when their children's teachers are prepared to come and visit them on their territory. Such home visits can be pivotal in establishing constructive working relationships with parents. They provide teachers with an opportunity to see the circumstances in which the family is living and enable them to meet other family members. Home visits provide an ideal opportunity for teachers to answer parents' questions and deal with any concerns they may have. In addition, home visits can enable teachers to find out how their pupils spend their time at home and how their parents manage their behavior (Grant & Ray 2010). The video clip, entitled, *Parent Teacher Home Visit* (Denver Public Schools 2016) shows how parent-teacher home visits build trust between teachers and families and help break down some of the barriers between them. The home visit is a voluntary meeting between two equal partners with the common goals of building strong and positive relationships between the family and the school and, as a result, create a better chance of success for students.

Attitudes and Beliefs on Working with Parents

A prerequisite for working with parents effectively is developing an understanding of family needs and priorities and being able to facilitate constructive working relationships with parents. Karen Mapp provides tips for improving family engagement in the video entitled *Dr. Karen Mapp Shares Advice for Educators on Family and Community Engagement Strategies* (Scholastic 2015). The suggestions include a focus on examining your beliefs about families and on what they can contribute. It is recommended that teachers emphasize positive news about what children are doing and focus on children's learning and what families can do to help.

Examples of PI and PE at Various Stages of the Education System

This brief video, entitled *FAST Introduction Video* (Families and Schools Together Inc. 2014) focuses on the benefits of engaging parents and families with schools. The video clip, entitled *Family Engagement = Student Success* (Learning Leaders 2011), involves several high-profile people to reinforce this message. It supports the importance of parent and family engagement in facilitating student success.

An interesting video from The New Zealand Educational Institute (2014), *Engaging parents in education*, focuses on parent engagement in New Zealand from early years to high school. It shows how a kindergarten, a primary school, and two secondary schools engage parents in their children's education. The schools have families from Chinese and Maori backgrounds, and teachers use the Maori terms "whanau," which refers to extended family, and "whakapapa," which refers to family heritage. A key focus in the video, at all levels, is the use of three-way parent/teacher/child meetings.

Early Years Examples

The importance of parent and family involvement is perhaps most obvious at the preschool level or in the early years of education. Encouraging parents to get involved in their children's education provides them with confidence in understanding how to facilitate their children's learning. This lays the foundation for their engagement throughout the years of schooling, as illustrated by the video, entitled *Every Parent Matters* (Lenclos 2009), which also demonstrates the importance of sharing learning goals.

Family involvement/engagement is an essential component of all effective forms of early childhood education that have demonstrated a wide range of positive outcomes. For example, the longest-running longitudinal study in early education, the Perry Preschool Study, has shown that investing in high-quality early education, including parent involvement, yields positive results for children and families. This longitudinal study found that at age 40, the participants who experienced the preschool program were more likely to have graduated from high school; had fewer teenage pregnancies; were more likely to hold a job and have higher earnings; committed fewer crimes; and were more likely to own their own home and car.

There are many other types of programs, one of the most enduring and well researched of which are Head Start programs that emerged over 50 years ago. The National Head Start Association (2017) explores the lives of Head Start students, parents, teachers, and alumni working to envision and create a better world for all, in a video entitled *The Head Start Advantage*. It focuses on the achievements of program graduates, on program goals, and emphasizes the need for support of parents and families and long-term outcomes in terms of the impressive return on every dollar invested.

Elementary School Examples

The video clip, entitled *The Power of Family-Teacher Partnerships* (Flamboyan Foundation 2011), focuses on the power of family-teacher partnerships and shows how teachers can create positive working relationships with parents at the elementary school level to address children's learning and behavioral challenges.

The next video, entitled *Parents as Partners: Engaging Families in Schools* (Children's Institute 2015), shows how the Parents as Partners program in a rural area of Oregon has been helping parents to connect with schools. It explains how the establishment of a family room within the school was helpful in breaking down barriers.

Middle School Examples

A video from National Network of Teachers of the Year (2015), *Building Relationships with Parents*, shows a teacher, who works part-time in a middle school, talking about the importance of building relationships with students, colleagues, and parents. She suggests meeting with parents where they feel most comfortable, whether at school, their homes, or somewhere in the local community.

The video, entitled *Parent Involvement Contributes to Results* (Schools that Work 2008), features a parent from a middle school in Atlanta who describes her involvement at the school and how it contributes to improved results for students. She shares that engaged parents have helped the school change from a chronically failing school to being the best in the district.

In the video, entitled *Relationship Building: Parent/Teacher Communication* (San Bernardino School District 2017), teachers at elementary and middle school levels describe several different ways of communicating effectively with parents.

High School Examples

The video clip, entitled *The Power of Parent and Teacher Partnership* (Families in Schools 2012) focuses on the power of parent-teacher partnership at the high school level at a school with many minority parents.

The final video clip from The Ottawa Catholic School Board (2015), entitled *The OCSB Family Welcome Centre: Parent Perspective*, illustrates how the involvement of mothers and fathers continues to be valuable at the high school level and how this is particularly important for families with different ethnic backgrounds or from different countries.

Conclusion

This chapter was based on the research finding that when teachers implement effective strategies for engaging parents, they will bring about improved outcomes for their students. The evidence-based research supporting parental engagement and its effectiveness in improving children's outcomes were considered. An effective model for parental engagement focusing on parents' needs and their potential contributions was presented. Practical strategies for implementing the model and developing effective working relationships with parents were outlined. Examples of parental engagement, illustrated by video clips, were provided in the early years, elementary, middle school, and high school levels.

References

Australian Institute for Teaching and School Leadership. (2016, April 21). *Leading parental engagement initiatives [Video]*. YouTube. https://www.youtube.com/watch?v=d5jBCRrPcao

Book Trust. (2011, September 30). *Everybody writes: Creating a school newsletter [Video]*. YouTube. https://www.youtube.com/watch?v=GEPfVtLnz9A

Children's Institute. (2015, April 28). *Parents as partners: Engaging families in schools [Video]*. YouTube. https://www.youtube.com/watch?v=dGEwYI9M0gc

Denver Public Schools. (2016, March 2). *Parent teacher home visit - Denver public schools (full version) [Video]*. YouTube. https://www.youtube.com/watch?v=qbCIpLt4OGo

Education Endowment Foundation. (2021, October 28). *Teaching and learning toolkit*. EEF. https://educationendowmentfoundation.org.uk/education-evidence/teaching-learning-toolkit

Epstein, J. L. (2000). *School, family and community partnerships*. Westview Press.

Epstein, J. L. (2018). School, family and community partnerships in teachers' professional work. *Journal of Education for Teaching, 44*(3), 397–406.

Every Person Influences Children NYC. (2010, March 12). *Part 2 - "On the same page - Families and schools as partners" [Video]*. YouTube. https://www.youtube.com/watch?v=lns-se2AZxM

Families in Schools. (2012, February 10). *The power of parent and teacher partnership [Video]*. YouTube. https://www.youtube.com/watch?v=vDiE2yGhzFc&t=68s

Families and Schools Together Inc. (2014, November 18). *FAST (families and schools together) introduction video [Video]*. YouTube. https://www.youtube.com/watch?v=N5qQXYfow6g

Flamboyan Foundation. (2011, November 18). *The power of family-teacher partnerships [Video]*. YouTube. https://www.youtube.com/watch?v=vNdwJTKuHDw

Goodall, J. (2013). Parental engagement to support children's learning: A six point model. *School Leadership & Management, 38*(2), 133–150.

Grant, K. B., & Ray, J. A. (2010). *Home, school and community collaboration: Culturally responsive family involvement*. Sage.

Hattie, J. (2009). *Visible learning: A synthesis of over 800 meta-analyses relating to achievement*. Routledge.

Henderson, A. T., & Mapp, K. L. (2002). *A new wave of evidence: The impact of school, family and community connections on student achievement*. Southwest Educational Development Laboratory.

Hornby, G. (2000). *Improving parental involvement*. Cassell.

Hornby, G. (2011). *Parental involvement in childhood education: Building effective school-family partnerships*. Springer.

Hornby, G., Hall, E., & Hall, C. (2003). *Counselling pupils in schools: Skills and strategies for teachers*. Routledge Falmer.

Hornby, G., & Lafaele, R. (2011). Barriers to parental involvement in education: An explanatory model. *Educational Review, 63*(1), 37–52.

Hornby, G., & Murray, R. (1983). Group programmes for parents of children with various handicaps. *Child: Care, Health and Development, 9*(3), 185–198.

Jeynes, W. H. (2005). A meta-analysis of the relation of parental involvement to urban elementary school student academic achievement. *Urban Education, 40*(3), 237–269.

Jeynes, W. H. (2007). The relation between parental involvement and urban secondary school student academic achievement: A meta-analysis. *Urban Education, 42*(1), 82–110.

Jeynes, W. H. (2018). A practical model for school leaders to encourage parental involvement and parental engagement. *School Leadership & Management, 38*(2), 147–163.

Julie Mazzolli Productions. (2014, April 25). *In charge: Student-led conferences [Video]*. YouTube. https://www.youtube.com/watch?v=TOP_7BzimMo

Kinney, P. (2005). Letting students take the lead. *Principal Leadership, 6*(2), 33–36.

Learning Leaders. (2011, March 11). *Family engagement = Student success [Video]*. YouTube. https://www.youtube.com/watch?v=gwEPv2ob_QI

Lenclos, M. (2009, April 29). *Every parent matters (clip) [Video]*. YouTube. https://www.youtube.com/watch?v=fPsUO4TeiDg

Little, N. & Allan, J. (1989). Student-led teacher parent conferences. *Elementary School Guidance and Counseling, 20*, 277–282.

Moriah College. (2018, August 22). *Primary school open day 2018 [Video]*. YouTube. https://www.youtube.com/watch?v=a4efref2UtA

National Head Start Association. (2017, August 3). *The head start advantage*. YouTube. https://www.youtube.com/watch?v=IBS-fcY4Tc8

National Network of Teachers of the Year. (2015, April 29). *Building relationships with parents [Video]*. YouTube. https://www.youtube.com/watch?v=aQqttDEVoZI

New Zealand Educational Institute. (2014, May 14). *Engaging parents in education [Video]*. YouTube. https://www.youtube.com/watch?v=6r60UuMYqkM

Northern California Public Media. (2016, January 12). *The importance of parental involvement [Video]*. YouTube. https://www.youtube.com/watch?v=F9ff3kdpuBw

Ottawa Catholic School Board. (2015, July 15). *The OCSB Family Welcome Centre: Parent Perspective [Video]*. YouTube. https://www.youtube.com/watch?v=XZiHqeSmSJI

Raise the Bar Parents. (2014, January 30). *Student led parent teacher conference - Middle school [Video]*. YouTube. https://www.youtube.com/watch?v=R9y2kEGnMR4

San Bernardino School District. (2017, October 4). *Relationship building: Parent/teacher communication [Video]*. YouTube. https://www.youtube.com/watch?v=LTKOhxE4LNc

Scholastic. (2015, September 15). *Dr. Karen Mapp shares advice for educators on family and community engagement strategies [Video]*. YouTube. https://www.youtube.com/watch?v=6j-Hkl5vIS4

Schools that Work. (2008, October 8). *Parent involvement contributes to results [Video]*. YouTube. https://www.youtube.com/watch?time_continue=15&v=UlXFz-Q2l5U&feature=emb_logo

Turnbull, A., Turnbull, R., Erwin, E. J., Soodak, L. C., & Shogren, K. A. (2011). *Families, professionals and exceptionality*. Pearson.

Wilder, S. (2014). Effects of parental involvement on academic achievement: A meta-synthesis. *Educational Review, 66*(3), 377–397.

Chapter 10
Implementation of Evidence-Based Teaching Strategies

Abstract The rationale for focusing on the implementation of evidence-based teaching strategies is that this is far more difficult than it first appears. It continues to be the source of much frustration among educators and other professionals who are committed to the philosophy of evidence-based practice. An example of this from the medical field, the long campaign to establish a protocol for handwashing before examining patients, is discussed as an illustration. This highlights the necessity for addressing typical barriers to the implementation of evidence-based teaching strategies, such as the mistrust that many teachers have of educational research, confusion created by use of terms such as "research informed," use of ineffective models of professional development, and the traditional culture of teaching found in many schools. It also highlights the need for making optimum use of various facilitating factors, including effective professional development for teachers, utilizing step-by-step processes for implementing evidence-based teaching strategies, and establishing communities of practice so that teachers can support one another in implementing and sustaining the use of evidence-based strategies.

Rationale for Focusing on Implementation

In 1847, Hungarian doctor Ignaz Semmelweis was appointed to one of the two obstetric clinics at the University of Vienna General Hospital. He collected data and found that maternal mortality rates were 16% in one clinic, which was staffed by doctors and medical students, compared to 7% in the other, which midwives staffed. He also noted that the doctors and students often went directly to the delivery room after performing autopsies, whereas the midwives were not involved in autopsies. Therefore, he hypothesized that something was being transmitted via the hands of doctors and students from the autopsy room to the delivery theatre that was leading to maternal deaths. Semmelweis therefore recommended that hands be scrubbed in a chlorinated lime solution after leaving the autopsy room before examining patients in the obstetric clinic. Following the implementation of this measure, the maternal mortality rate fell dramatically to 3% in the clinic staffed by doctors and students and remained low thereafter.

So, one would think that after Semmelweis had established that washing and sterilizing hands saved lives, he would be congratulated and that this evidence-based practice would become standard practice in the hospital where he worked. But this was not the case, as many doctors refused to comply with the practice, and Semmelweis became unpopular for continuing to recommend it. He subsequently lost his job and was later admitted to a mental hospital, where he eventually died.

However, news of Semmelweis' research gradually spread throughout the international medical community. By the early 1900s, a medical researcher at one of the top medical schools in the USA had become an advocate for the evidence-based practice of thorough handwashing before performing surgery. He campaigned for this to be made a standard practice for around 30 years but is reported to have had little success (Slavin 2008). Many years later, in 1996, the CDC/Healthcare Infection Control Practices Advisory Committee in the USA recommended that either antimicrobial soap or a waterless antiseptic agent be used for cleansing hands before examining patients. Surprisingly, even after this directive, a study conducted in one teaching university hospital in the USA in 2007 found that staff handwashing between examining patients in intensive care units had an overall compliance rate of just 54%.

The point of this account of the campaign to establish handwashing protocols for doctors is that it took many years after the discovery that washing and sterilizing hands was saving lives for this evidence-based practice to become mandated. Also, even after it was established as an evidence-based practice, its implementation is still far from universal. The relevance of this to the field of education is that it is not enough to simply identify teaching strategies that are evidence-based practices and then expect them to be implemented widely in schools. Instead, it is expected that it may be a long and frustrating process to reach a point where evidence-based teaching strategies are widespread in schools. Therefore, it is important to recognize the potential barriers to implementation and the facilitating factors that can be utilized to adopt the most effective approaches for encouraging and supporting evidence-based teaching strategies. This chapter discusses common barriers to, and facilitating factors for, implementing and sustaining evidence-based teaching strategies in schools.

Barriers to the Use of Evidence-Based Strategies

There are several common barriers to using evidence-based strategies in schools that need to be overcome if these are to be successfully implemented. A major barrier to the widespread implementation of evidence-based teaching strategies is the mistrust that many teachers have of educational research, which is the major source of evidence-based practices (Brown 2013; Cook & Cook 2011). There has been a long-standing view of teachers that educational research has little to tell them about how to teach effectively (Oancea 2005). This has led to a gap between educational research and practice that has been difficult to overcome (Cain & Allan 2017; Cook et al. 2008). Traditionally, teachers have looked to experienced practitioners and existing practice in schools as their major sources of information about effective teaching strategies. Therefore, to get teachers to abandon their traditional means of determining which instructional strategies to use, they first need to be convinced about the value of evidence-based strategies in improving student outcomes and begin to view research studies as reliable indicators of what works best with students.

Another major barrier to the implementation of evidence-based strategies is confusion over the meaning of terms such as "best practice," "research-based," and "research informed," which are often used synonymously with "evidence-based practice." However, they refer to quite different things, as noted in Chap. 1. For example, many teachers may transfer the cynicism they have toward the term "best practice," which has in the past been used to recommend strategies that have not necessarily had strong evidence bases, to strategies now shown to be evidence-based practices (Cook & Cook 2011). Alternatively, teachers may assume that interventions referred to as "research informed" are underpinned by solid research evidence, which need not be the case. This contrasts with evidence-based practices, which by definition must have extensive high-quality research evidence of their effectiveness and clear evidence of a magnitude of effect sufficient to impact students' lives meaningfully. "Research informed" can mean just about anything, including being based on research of dubious quality disseminated by promoters of recommended interventions in which they have a vested interest. Such is the case for interventions that are not evidence-based, such as Irlen lenses, as discussed in Chap. 1. Therefore, teachers must clearly understand what evidence-based practice actually means and how it is different from other terms that sound similar. It is necessary before they can be expected to commit to using them in their classrooms.

Yet another major barrier is that the professional development provided for teachers on evidence-based strategies is often considered ineffective (Houchins, Shippen & Murphy 2012; Odom 2009). The most widely used model, the "one-off workshop" in which information about teaching strategies or programs is presented, is generally regarded to have little impact on the instructional strategies that teachers subsequently use, especially if there is no ongoing support for the use of these strategies (George & Childs 2012).

A further barrier is a traditional culture of teaching in many schools, where existing practices that have been used for many years are the norm. This makes the implementation of strategies based on research evidence regarding effective practices very difficult. Clearly, many practitioners will need help with implementing evidence-based strategies, and some of the educational research literature can offer suggestions but with the understanding that these answers will always be influenced by cultural appropriateness and availability of professional wisdom, as noted in Chap. 1. With this in mind some important facilitators for the implementation of evidence-based practices are suggested below.

Factors Facilitating the Use of Evidence-Based Teaching Strategies

Learning about the eight key evidence-based teaching strategies is just the first component in implementing evidence-based practice to improve student outcomes. Other factors facilitate the implementation of these in schools.

First, developing a thorough understanding of the rationales for and theory underpinning each of the eight key evidence-based teaching strategies is essential before attempting to use them. This can be achieved by reading the text of the relevant chapter in this book and clarifying any confusion by further reading or talking with a colleague who is experienced in using the strategy before trying it out. This will avoid any misunderstandings about the strategy undermining its use, resulting in disappointing outcomes. A common example occurs with cooperative learning when teachers focus on the aspect of organizing students to work in small groups without ensuring the presence of the individual accountability and positive interdependence that are essential for its success, as explained in Chap. 5.

A second facilitating factor is the opportunity to observe colleagues or other teachers experienced in using one of the eight key evidence-based teaching strategies and implementing the strategy in the classroom. This is the reason why several videos demonstrating the use of the key strategies are identified and linked in the text of each chapter. This enables teachers to see how experienced teachers implement the strategies and to observe their impact on students. The advantage of watching the videos over live demonstrations is that these can be viewed repeatedly so that teachers have time to take in all necessary aspects of the implementation.

A third facilitating factor is the use of professional wisdom acquired through relevant experience, being used to adapt evidence-based strategies for specific students, classes, and school environments while maintaining key components and thereby the fidelity of the interventions (Cook & Cook 2011).

The fourth facilitating factor is the use of a stepped or sequenced process to ensure effective implementation. For example, as Cook, Tankersley, and Harjusola-Webb (2008) suggested, the first step is identifying and obtaining information about evidence-based strategies consistent with what they are trying to achieve. Next is selecting the appropriate evidence-based strategies for their student's learning needs, considering teachers' strengths and experiences, matching these to the educational environment, and adapting the strategies as necessary. Next, it is crucial to ensure effective teaching practices in classrooms where evidence-based strategies are introduced. Finally, it is essential to regularly monitor student progress and adapt evidence-based strategies, or select new ones, as necessary.

The fifth facilitating factor for implementing evidence-based teaching strategies is the delivery of effective professional development for teachers. Odom (2009) has proposed that "enlightened" professional development includes several key aspects. First, team-building and collaboration need to be built into the process. Second, consultants or coaches should provide demonstrations of the evidence-based strategies in classroom settings and follow-up, with feedback to teachers on their use of the interventions. Third, teachers should form communities of practice (see below) to share information and reflections on introducing evidence-based strategies into their classrooms. Fourth, online resources, such as video clips of evidence-based strategies used in classroom settings, including ones linked in this book, can be accessed to provide helpful information and guidelines on their use. Fifth, web-based video and interactive systems, such as wikis and video feedback, can be used to assist the implementation of evidence-based strategies.

Therefore, besides the need for effective professional development and step-by-step processes for implementing evidence-based teaching strategies, it is also vital for the successful use and maintenance of these interventions that teachers have support in using them (Torres, Farley & Cook 2012). This needs to come from school principals or head teachers and teachers' colleagues (Cain & Allan 2017). As suggested above, schools should establish a community of practice so teachers can support one another in using evidence-based strategies. They can then share their experiences and produce "practice-based evidence" to monitor and evaluate the effectiveness of the interventions in their particular settings.

The term "community of practice" was proposed by Wenger (2000), who pointed out that learning occurs when people interact and that human beings have always formed communities in which knowledge is shared. He suggested that communities of practice can support professional practitioners in developing shared understandings, thereby playing an important role in facilitating professional learning. Communities of practice are collaborative networks that generate a supportive culture that fosters trust and acceptance among group members, enabling individuals to reflect on the experience and grow their knowledge. The psychological safety within them supports participants to be willing to take risks and try new things as part of their growth and learning. Therefore, participating in communities of practice is valuable for teachers to facilitate learning about evidence-based teaching strategies, enabling their implementation and ensuring their sustained use over time.

Sustaining the Use of Evidence-Based Teaching Strategies

A widely used whole-school evidence-based strategy is Positive Behavioral Interventions and Supports (PBIS), discussed in Chap. 8, Functional Behavioral Analysis. The PBIS approach has been taken up in many countries around the world and has considerable research support for effectively creating positive classroom behavior management systems and reducing student behavioral difficulties (Fox et al. 2021). However, one review of PBIS reported that 33% of schools no longer use it 5 years after its first implementation, which is why a recent review of studies on PBIS carried out an analysis to find out the key factors related to ensuring its sustainability.

In their review, Fox et al. (2021) discovered that schools that maintained it had paid particular attention to variables such as monitoring the fidelity of key aspects of PBIS in its implementation and ensuring the adequacy of the resources required for it to be effective. These schools had made sure that there was widespread "buy-in" from teachers to the PBIS philosophy at the start of the project and that this was maintained within the PBIS implementation team by continued support from school leadership. The PBIS team continually focused on ensuring data-driven interventions and adjusted the organization of PBIS to make sure that it aligned to the school's unique context. Finally, although there had been extensive training of teachers on PBIS on its initial implementation, there was ongoing training available to train any new staff who joined the school.

These factors are consistent with the three overlapping elements required for the effective implementation of evidence-based practices outlined in Chap. 1. Effective evidence-based practices occur at the convergence of extensive research evidence of meaningful change, relevant teacher wisdom and skills, and consistency with school and community cultures. The above review of PBIS reminds us that these three components need to be present for the successful implementation and sustainability of evidence-based teaching strategies.

Conclusion

This book has made a case for implementing evidence-based practice in education, with a particular focus on eight key evidence-based teaching strategies. Frustration with the speed of progress toward establishing the evidence-based approach at all levels of education systems has been noted, and explanations have been made about why this is and how it can be changed. It has been suggested that improving educational outcomes for all learners will require overcoming barriers to the use of evidence-based strategies, thereby facilitating the widespread implementation of the eight key evidence-based strategies. Individual teachers and schools can achieve much; however, teacher education also has an important role to play in this. New teachers and practicing teachers need to learn how to identify evidence-based strategies and implement them effectively while avoiding using those that lack evidence, even if they are popular. This will ensure that effective teaching strategies are embedded in the daily practice of teachers and schools.

This book can be used in initial teacher education and in-service training of teachers at all levels, from early childhood education through secondary school teaching to help teachers implement evidence-based practice. Additionally, the book is designed for individual teachers or small groups of teachers, at any stage of their careers, to enhance their knowledge of evidence-based strategies and provide guidance on implementing these in their classrooms. It is intended that using the book in this way and formal teacher education and training will lead to teaching becoming a more evidence-based profession, which will result in improved educational outcomes at all levels of education systems.

References

Brown, C. (2013). *Making evidence matter: A new perspective for evidence-informed policy making in education*. Institute of Education Press.

Cain, T., & Allan, D. (2017). The invisible impact of educational research. *Oxford Review of Education, 43*(6), 718–732.

Cook, B. G., & Cook, S. C. (2011). Unraveling evidence-based practices in special education. *Journal of Special Education, 47*(2), 71–82.

Cook, B. G., Tankersley, M., & Harjusola-Webb, S. (2008). Evidence-based special education and professional wisdom: Putting it all together. *Intervention in School and Clinic, 44*(2), 105–111.

Fox, R., Leif, E., Moore, D., Furlonger, B., Anderson, A., & Sharma, U. (2021). A systematic review of the facilitators and barriers to the sustained implementation of school-wide positive behavioral interventions and supports. *Education and Treatment of Children*. https://doi.org/10.1007/s43494-021-00056-0

George, H. P., & Childs, K. E. (2012). Evaluating implementation of school-wide behaviour support: Are we doing it well? *Preventing School Failure, 56*(4), 197–206.

Houchins, D. E., Shippen, M. E., & Murphy, K. M. (2012). Evidence-based professional development considerations along the school-to-prison pipeline. *Teacher Education and Special Education, 35*(4), 271–283.

Oancea, A. (2005). Criticisms of educational research: Key topics and levels of analysis. *British Educational Research Journal, 31*(2), 157–183.

Odom, S. L. (2009). The tie that binds: Evidence-based practice, implementation science, and outcomes for children. *Topics in Early Childhood Special Education, 29*(1), 53–61.

Slavin, R. E. (2008). Evidence-based reform in education: What will it take? *European Educational Research Journal, 7*(1), 124–128.

Torres, C., Farley, C. A., & Cook, B. G. (2012). A special educator's guide to successfully implementing evidence-based practices. *Teaching Exceptional Children, 45*(1), 64–73.

Wenger, E. (2000). Communities of practice and social learning systems. *Organization, 7*(2), 225–246.

Index

A

Ability grouping, 3–5, 7
Active listening, 16, 19, 20, 28
Advanced cooperative interactions, 65
Anticipation guides, 101
Assertion skills, 16, 20

B

Base groups, 72
Basics of Cooperative Learning (video), 63
Behavior contract functions, 116
Behavior intervention plan (BIP), 114
    implementing, 114
    monitoring, 114
    teacher monitors, 115
    visual schedules, 115
Best Evidence Encyclopedia, 4, 5, 9
Blind drawing, 68

C

Circle time, 3
Class-wide peer tutoring, 89, 90
Community of practice, 137
Concept mapping, 96, 97
Cooperative engagements, 69
Cooperative learning, 4, 9, 10, 103
    definition, 63
    effective class-wide interventions, 63
    evidence-based teaching strategy, 64
    face-to-face interaction, 67–68
    features, 78
    fundamental elements, 63
    group processing, 70

    individual accountability, 66–67
    intervention strategies, 64
    planning (*see* Planning, cooperative
      learning)
    positive impacts, 65
    positive interdependence, 65–66
    primary developers, 63
    research studies, 64
    social skills, 68–70
    theory, 64
Cooperative learning strategies
    elementary students
      four corners, 76, 77
      numbered heads together, 75, 76
    middle and high school students
      group investigation, 78
      jigsaw, 77
      STAD, 77, 78
Cooperative strategies, 63
Cooperative teaching and learning, 65
Cooperative work, 73
Criterion-based assessment, 38
Curriculum-based assessments, 36

D

Demonstration and modeling, 55
Describe, Express (and/or Explain), Specify
      and Consequences (DESC)
      script, 21, 22
Descriptive assessments, 112
DI lesson
    demonstration and modeling, 54, 55
    feedback and verification, 56, 57
    guided practices, 55, 56

DI lesson (*cont.*)
    independent practice, 56
    scaffolded instruction, 53, 54
    setting learning intention, 53
DI planning
    engaging students, 52
    older students needs adaptation, 52
    students' existing knowledge and
        skills, 51, 52
Direct Instruction (DI), 9, 10, 103
    classroom practices, 49
    dependent, 60
    explicit, 60
    historical development, 46
    lessons (*see* DI lesson)
    NIFDI's website, 47
    planning (*see* DI planning)
    principles, 48
    published programs, 47
    rationale, 45
    teacher interventions, 60
    teaching practices, 45
Direct Instructional System for Teaching and
        Remediation (DISTAR), 47
DI strategies
    middle and high school students
        explicit instruction, 60
        scaffolding with socratic circles, 59, 60
    preschool and elementary students
        Reading Recovery, 58, 59
        shared reading, 59

E
Education Endowment Foundation (EEF), 5
Effective instruction, 48
Effective peer tutoring teams building
    appropriate sharing climate, 87
    clarifying tutoring methods, 88
    establishing learning structures, 87
    learning outcomes, 87, 88
    monitoring progress and providing
        feedback, 88, 89
    sense of shared purpose, 86
Effective teaching, 48
Emotional experiences, 55
Empathy, 16, 17, 27, 28
Entrance tickets, 41
Evidence-based behavior management, 105
Evidence-based practices, 49, 134
Evidence-based strategies, 134, 135
    barrier, 135
    factor, 136
    high-quality research, 135

    learning, 136
    teachers, 135
Evidence-based teaching, 134, 136, 137
Evidence-based teaching strategies
    ability grouping, 7
    best practice, 3
    classrooms, 3
    education, 2, 9, 10
    effect sizes, 4, 6–8
    feedback, 5
    field of education, 2, 4
    flipped classroom approach, 3
    formative assessment/evaluation,
        3–5, 9, 10
    implementation, 2
    interventions, 2–5
    Irlen lenses, 8, 9
    learning styles, 8
    literacy and numeracy, 1
    medicine and agriculture, 1
    metacognition, 5
    methodological grounds, 2
    research-based, 2
    research-informed, 3
    school and community cultures, 4
    setting, 5, 7, 9
    streaming, 5, 7
    teachers, 2
Exit tickets, 41
Explicit instruction, 60

F
Face-to-face interactions, 67, 68
Facilitative communication, 3
Family involvement, 129
Family-teacher partnerships, 130
Feedback, 56, 57
Flipped classroom, 3
Formal groups, 72
Formative assessment, 53, 103
    checklists, 41, 42
    computer assessment programs, 33
    cooperative learning strategies, 38
    criterion-based assessments, 38
    critical planning tool, 31
    developmental sponges, 39
    entrance and exit tickets, 41
    evaluations, 31
    evidence-based practice, 32
    evidence-based strategies, 32
    experiential learning, 39
    feedback, 31
    frequency, 34

instructional cycle, 32
knowledge, 31
learning, 32, 35
middle and high school students, 40
observation, 36
performance feedback, 33
planning, 34
questioning, 37
rubrics, 40
self-reflection, 37, 38
skills, 31
student products, 31
teaching, 32
timing, 34
Four corners strategy, 76, 77
Functional analysis, 112
Functional behavior assessment (FBA), 107,
        110, 117
    behavioral intervention
            systems, 106
    classroom dynamics, 105
    classroom learning environment, 105
    components, 111
    conducting, 111
    engagement, 109
    functioning classroom, 107
    inappropriate behavior, 107
    incorporating, 111
    interventions, 107
    national policies, 106
    proactive management plans, 108
    school-wide level, 108
    teacher participation, 111
    teachers and students, 108, 109
    trust, 110
Functional behavioral analysis, 9

G
Genuineness, 16, 17, 28
Give One, Get One activity, 69
Graphic organizers, 96, 100, 103
Group investigation, 78
Group leadership skills, 16, 27, 28
Group processing, 70
Group sharing, 66
Guided practices, 39, 55, 56

H
Head Start programs, 129
Home-school reading programs, 125
Home visits, 128

I
"I do, we do, you do", 54, 60
Incredible Years programs, 26
Independent practice, 49, 56
Indirect assessments, 113
Individual accountability, 63
    active participation and motivation, 64
    definition, 66
    group recitation, 67
    group study with random checking, 67
    practicing through activities, 67
    projects and assignments, 66
    student's performance assessment, 64
Individual support, 110
Informal groups, 72
Interdependent peer tutoring models, 84
Irlen lenses, 8, 9

J
Jigsaw strategy, 77

K
KWL method, 100, 101

L
Ladder of Feedback guideline, 86
Leadership assignments, 69
Learner-centered approach, 16
Learning intentions, 53
Learning styles, 5, 8
Lev Vygotsky's zones of proximal
            development, 64–65
Listening skills, 16, 17, 23, 27, 28

M
Mastery learning, 46
Math sequence, 85
Message relay activities, 69
Meta-analyses, 4, 5, 9
Metacognition, 96
Metacognitive strategies, 9
    average effect size, 95
    encouraging students, 103
    extensive evidence, 95
    study skills (*see* Study skills)
    theory, 96
    training, 95
    types, 102
Mnemonics, 97, 98

N

National Institute for Direct Instruction
(NIFDI), 47
Non-Direct Instruction programs, 46
Note-taking, 96, 99

P

Paraphrasing, 16, 17, 19
Parental contributions
children, 125
education, 125
teachers, 125
time and ability, 125
Parental engagement
barriers, 122
beliefs, 122
childhood, 121
children, 124
communication, 128
in education, 122
family engagement, 122, 129
guidelines, 126
home visits, 128
informal events, 126
and parental involvement, 121
parents need, 123
parent-teacher factors, 122
parent-teacher interviews, 126
parent-teacher meetings, 126, 127
prerequisite, 128
school and home, 126
schools type, 122
supportive counseling, 124
telephone, 127
theoretical model, 123
written communication, 127
Parent education, 124
Parent-teacher association, 124
Parent-teacher partnership, 130
Parking lot, 68
Passive listening, 16–19
Peer editing, 91, 92
Peer tutoring, 9, 10
interactions, 83
learning process, 92
models, 84
planning
activities and work products, 85, 86
clear functioning criteria, 84, 85
student's role play, 85
students' academic performance
reports, 83

teams building (*see* Effective peer tutoring
teams building)
theory, 84
Peer tutoring strategies
elementary students
class-wide, 89, 90
reciprocal, 90
secondary students
PALS, 90, 91
peer editing, 91, 92
Peer-assisted learning strategies
(PALS), 90, 91
Perry Preschool Study, 129
Planning, cooperative learning
establishing work habits and behaviors
expectations and routines
modeling, 73, 74
making cooperative learning
strategies, 75
setting norms/rules, 74
group forming factors
individual and group expectations, 73
knowledge and skills scope and
depth, 73
size, 72
task complexity, 73
grouping types
base groups, 72
formal, 72
informal, 72
learning experiences, 70
rewarding, cooperative environment, 73
selecting assignments
elementary students, 71
hints, 71
preschool students, 71
secondary students, 72
Positive behavioral interventions and supports
(PBIS), 137
implementation, 138
organization, 138
review, 138
Positive interdependence, 63
achieving learning goals, 64
climate, 65
group sharing, 66
group work, 64
individual members, 65
positive attitudes development, 65
role-playing, 66
sense of belonging, 65
Practice-based evidence, 137
Primary-aged students, 57

Prior learning, 52
"Project Follow Through", 46
Published DI programs
    materials, 47, 61
    reading skills teaching, 47
    scaffolds, 47
    types, 47
    visual charts, 47

R

*Reading Mastery Training Series: Video 1_*
    Path to Literacy (Video), 48
Reading Recovery, 6, 58, 59
Reciprocal learning exchanges, 92
Reciprocal peer tutoring, 90
Reciprocal teaching, 99, 100
Rehearsal, 96
Respect, 16, 17, 27
Rewarding, 73
Role-playing, 66
Rubrics, 37, 40

S

Scaffolded instruction, 48, 53, 54, 59
Scaffolded learning, 48
Scaffolding strategies, 54
School-wide behavior management, 106
Self-awareness, 96
Self-reflection, 96
Semantic mapping, 96
Semmelweis' research, 134
Shared learning experience, 84
Shared reading, 59
Social and emotional learning (SEL), 27, 28
Social skills
    cooperative climate, 68
    encouraging activities
        Give One, Get One, 69
        leadership assignments, 69
        message relay activities, 69
    interaction and self-management, 68
    participation, 69
    respect for others, 69
    social-emotional and academic learning, 68
    turn-taking, 69
SPARK framework, 85
SQ3R reading method, 98
Student-directed approach, 41
Student-led parent-teacher meeting, 127
Student-teacher game, 116
Student Teams Achievement Divisions
    (STAD), 77, 78

Student-to-teacher ratios, 79
Study skills
    anticipation guides, 101
    concept mapping, 96, 97
    KWL, 100, 101
    learning skills, 96
    mnemonics, 97, 98
    reciprocal teaching, 99, 100
    SQ3R reading method, 98
    think aloud, 101, 102

T

Teacher-focused instruction, 46
Teacher moderation, 89
Teacher-student rapport
    academic and social outcomes, 17
    active listening, 19, 20
    aggression, 23, 24
    assertion muscle levels, 21
    assertion skills, 20
    attentiveness, 17
    classrooms, 15
    constructive feedback, 21, 22
    cooperative learning, 17
    evidence-based practice, 15
    high-quality, 16
    interpersonal skills, 16
    learner-centered approach, 16
    paraphrasing, 19
    passive listening, 18
    peer tutoring, 17
    physical assertiveness, 20
    problem-solving, 24
    responding to criticism, 22, 23
    SEL, 16, 27, 28
    skills, 17
    social and emotional development, 25–27
    social and emotional outcomes, 15
    teacher interpersonal behaviors, 15
    vocal assertiveness, 21
Teacher-student relationships, 9, 10, 15,
    16, 28
Teaching and cognitive strategies, 48
Teaching and Learning Toolkit, 4, 5,
    7–9, 31
Teaching interventions, 48
Teaching script, 47
Team-building, 136
Text messaging, 128
Think aloud, 101, 102
Think-pair-share, 38, 75
Tiered systems of intervention, 106
Time and resource management, 96

U
U.S. Department of Education, 5
U.S. Department of Education and Office of
    Economic Opportunity, 46

V
Visual charts, 47, 52

W
What Works Clearinghouse, 4–6, 9
Whole-school approach, 106

Z
Zone of Proximal Development, 55

Printed in Great Britain
by Amazon

53785501R00097